I0867058

The Treadmill Affect

The Treadmill Affect:
Marxism, Subjectivity, and the Present

Benjamin Lee

PRICKLY
PARADIGM
PRESS

Prickly Paradigm Press, LLC

5751 S. Woodlawn Ave.

Chicago, IL 60637

www.prickly-paradigm.com

ISBN: 9781734643572

Library of Congress Control Number: 2025932969

Printed in the United States of America on acid-free paper.

Contents

Introduction

Lauren Berlant's *Cruel Optimism* is one of the most important and incisive critiques of contemporary neoliberalism. The book defines its eponymous concept as "when something you desire is actually an obstacle to your flourishing" (Berlant 2011,1). Already a classic in literary studies, its theoretical framework drew upon the linguistic turn, Marxist literary criticism, gender studies, and contemporary affect theory, and has inspired many interpretations in and contributions to these varied fields. This pamphlet explores what a Marxist approach to a linguistic semiotics of affect and subjectivity might look like. In so doing, it attempts to revive the linguistic turn, which played a crucial role in the separation of "two cultures" of the natural sciences and humanities that persists to this day.

The answer will be found in the connections between Berlant's work and the work of two other intellectuals at the University of Chicago whom Berlant knew for over thirty years: the Marxist theorist Moishe Postone and the linguistic anthropologist Michael Silverstein. Postone, along with David Harvey, was one of the leading American Marxist theorists; in 1993, he wrote *Time, Labor, and Social Domination: A Reinterpretation of Marx's Critical Theory* and developed a unique interpretation of Marx that has become increasingly influential, especially in Europe as a part of Wertkritik. Silverstein was one of the last students of Russian linguist Roman Jakobson and combined Peircean semiotics with structural linguistics; his explorations into pragmatics and metapragmatics had inspired several generations of linguistic anthropologists and continued Jakobson's linguistic turn. All were also program directors at the Center for Psychosocial Studies (now the Center for Transcultural Studies) and frequent participants at center seminars and conferences. Although they had many graduate students in common and were friendly colleagues, they never collaborated in an official capacity.

This pamphlet starts with a problem that each of them faced in their own research but didn't see as an overarching problem for the social sciences and the humanities: time. Our modern Western notion of time includes two contradictory notions. One is *mathematical time*, which is abstract, infinitely divisible, reversible, and the framework of all events. Today, mathematical time is standardized by the regular vibrations of a cesium atom. The other is *duration*, the flow of time from future to present and past, which is irreversible and a function of events. Verbal tense is an example from everyday speech. This contrast between mathematical time and what Newton also called "duration" came to a head in a famous Paris debate in 1921 between the physicist Albert Einstein and the philosopher Henri Bergson. On the hundredth anniversary of the debate, the Economist wrote about the implications of the contradictory nature of time:

> At stake is not just the momentous question of what time is. The debate was a key event in the separation of sciences and humanities into what C. P. Snow, a British novelist, later called "two cultures." Einstein saw science as "the ultimate arbiter of truth," says Jimena Canales, author of "The Physicist and the Philosopher," a book about the episode. Bergson insisted that science did not have the last word. Their clash, Ms Canales says, raised the question, "What is the relation between the subjective

> and the objective, and can we have a form of knowledge that includes both?" (*The Economist*, April 9, 2022)

The ruckus about time created the split between subjectivity and objectivity that affected the whole modern worldview. In the academy, it was responsible for the split between contemporary social sciences and humanities, as expected utility and decision making under uncertainty had dominated the former and contemporary affect theory (of which Bergson was a major figure) had swept the latter.

Time was and remains a crucial problem for Marxism, literary cultural studies, and linguistic anthropology. In Marxism, time was measured by Newtonian abstract time, which was the mathematical time, in order to produce a commodity. In the linguistic turn, time was at the heart of the definition of the linguistic sign, including the divisions between semantics and pragmatics or Saussure's demarcation between *langue* (grammar) and *parole* (indexicality). For affect theory, time is in the gap between means-end reasoning dominant in the social sciences and a "flow" model of duration that came from Bergson and was popular in the humanities.

This pamphlet will use the contradiction between mathematical time and duration as a framework to analyze the relationship between time and subjectivity. It will start with Benedict Anderson, one of Berlant's mentors at Cornell, who asked whether a new kind of nationalist subjectivity arose out of the rhetorical and narrative genres of novels and newspapers in an expanding global print capitalism. He famously maintained that national subjectivity, *we the people*, moved in the "homogenous, empty time" of modern capitalism. At the end it will extend the work of Berlant, Postone, and Silverstein to give a "flow" model of affect and subjectivity that is an alternative to decision making and means-end reasoning.

Postone used "homogenous, empty time" as one end of the dialectic of abstract and concrete labor times that underlay Marx's account of value and capitalism. According to Postone, the dialectic of time led to the "treadmill" structure of technological innovation, which was also the affective structure of cruel optimism. The fetish translated value into subjectivity, which both Anderson and Berlant agreed was made possible through the rhetorical genres of realistic narration. Silverstein said that the Western notion of time came from language and there was a continuum of rhetorical tropes ordered by the contradiction of time, ranging from direct speech to third-person omniscient narration. Berlant chose two rhetorical tropes, apostrophe and free indirect style, to show how their interaction produced the affects peculiar to capitalism, including cruel optimism. Throughout *Cruel Optimism*, Berlant drew upon Bergson's duration, the flow of time from future to present and past, to create an alternative model of subjectivity dominant in the social sciences, which was decision making under uncertainty that came from expected utility and game theory. These two models of subjectivity are based on the contradiction in time that C. P. Snow described as responsible for the "two cultures" of the natural sciences and humanities.

Berlant confronted the problem of time up front. She maintained that there was an explanatory gap between abstract theoretical social science concepts (like Marxist notions of value) and the phenomenological reality of the *historical present* where affect lay; affect had an *indexical* relation to the event or situation in which it occurred. Affect was depicted in historical novels but had minimal explanatory value in Marxist accounts that used transhistorical concepts. Therefore, Postone's *Labor, Time, and Social Domination* was an *immanent critique* of Marx's volume I of *Capital*. An immanent critique was a sociohistorically specific account of capitalism that used native concepts to approach Berlant's *historical present*; it was like an ethnography that used local social and cultural categories.

This pamphlet starts with the same question that Berlant raised in *Cruel Optimism*. How do you close the temporal gap between Marxist theoretical explanations that abstract from the time of the *historical present*? Cruel optimism was "a deictic" (Berlant 2011, 27) or indexical; it overlapped with Postone's immanent critique of the *historical present* and Silverstein's *metapragmatics*, which was an account of indexicality. In *Cruel Optimism*, Berlant said that one of the major problems in Marxist explanations was analyzing the *historical present* with theoretical concepts that abstracted from the indexicality of the contemporary:

> Situated squarely within the mainstream tradition of Marxian cultural theory, even formidable critics like Harry Harootunian and Moishe Postone argue for seeing the present as an effect of historical forces that cannot be known fully by the presently living, who require scholarly and political education toward comprehending the structural and the systemic. Otherwise the present is cast as virtually ahistorical, fleeting, fantasmatic, or a space of symptomatic pseudoactivity. (Berlant 2011, 64)

In what follows, I explore this point of departure through a number of interconnected routes. The first two chapters give a brief history of the linguistic turn and Berlant's question to her mentor Benedict Anderson: How were new social affects created out of the narrative genres of novels and newspapers in a globalizing capitalism? Partial answers were provided by Postone and Silverstein, described in the following chapters. The tropes and genres they proposed make up a continuum from direct speech to free indirect style and indirect discourse that is temporally ordered by the same contradiction in time as value (abstract and concrete labor times); the fetish translated value into these tropes and genres, which created new social imaginaries like nationalism, the public sphere, and the market. Berlant aligned language with rhetorical "indirection" and selected apostrophe and free indirect style from the continuum to create the social affect of cruel optimism.

1
Historical Background

The linguistic turn strongly influenced the social sciences and humanities after World War II. At the beginning of a fifty-year arc, structuralism emphasized the objective perspective on language and seemed to unify anthropology, psychology, and linguistics under the rubric of uncovering the "structure of the human mind." The subjective perspective reacted to a "scientific" structuralism with its formulation of poststructuralism, in which linguistics had to pay more attention to the rhetorical and poetic functions of language. It joined with postmodernism in criticizing the progress of technology and modernity. The objective and subjective sides settled for a truce that continues to this day with the division of "two cultures" of science and humanities.

The "two cultures" division was repeated in Marxism. Macroeconomics criticized Marxism as nonscientific, but it was internalized by "structural Marxists" like the French philosopher Louis Althusser, who brandished the linguistic tools of structuralism to criticize the Hegelian tradition as not formal and objective (accusing it of being "dialectical" and nonscientific). Against a scientific Marxism, poststructuralist thinkers like Jacques Derrida, Paul De Man, and Gayatri Spivak emphasized the rhetorical perspectives in analyzing Marx, fissuring again into "two cultures," one facing computational linguistics and artificial intelligence and the other contemporary affect theory.

This pamphlet is an intervention among Marxist theory, the linguistic turn, and contemporary affect theory. It uses the tradition of many linguists who were interested in rhetoric and poetry to formulate a notion of "metapragmatics" to overcome the split between "objective" and "subjective" perspectives on language. Instead of logically analyzing language, metapragmatics showed the connection between language and larger social and cultural processes; language was the missing variable in the contradiction of mathematical time and duration embodied in the Marxian concept of value. The contradiction created the structure of relative surplus value, which provided the dynamic of Postone's treadmill structure and "immanent critique" of capitalism. The fetish translated the treadmill structure of relative surplus value into the rhetorical and narrative genres that made up the linguistic community from which new social affects like cruel optimism emerged.

The linguistic turn began when the anthropologist Claude Levi-Strauss and the linguist Roman Jakobson met as exiled intellectuals at the New School in New York City during World War II. Levi-Strauss sat in on Jakobson's course on phonology, and they would eventually coauthor an analysis of Baudelaire's *Les Chats*. Jakobson convinced Levi-Strauss to write *The Elementary Structures of Kinship* (1949), and structuralism was born. Levi-Strauss became the chair of social anthropology at the Collège de France in 1959 and cofounder of *l'Homme* with the linguist Benveniste. Later on, the developmental psychologist Jean Piaget and the linguist Noam Chomsky joined Levi-Strauss to form a triumvirate across psychology, linguistics, and anthropology.

At Royaumont, France, in 1958, there was a meeting of analytic and continental philosophers about language. It included a stellar cast of mostly Oxford philosophers including John Austin, R. M. Hare, Gilbert Ryle, Peter Strawson, Charles Taylor, Bernard Williams, and the American philosopher W.

V. Quine; continental philosophy was represented by H. L. Van Breda, Maurice Merleau-Ponty, and Jean Wahl. Although Charles Taylor wrote that the meeting was an example of failed communication, it introduced John Austin to French audiences, and his speech act philosophy became the bridge between analytic and continental philosophies. Benveniste published a series of articles on subjectivity and performativity (1972) that would initiate the turn to indexicality and *discours* in French linguistics, and Derrida's response to Austin, "Signature, Event, Context," which would catalyze poststructuralist interests in performativity that survived in literary cultural studies and philosophy by such thinkers as Eve Sedgwick and Judith Butler.

Although the Royaumont conference was considered a failure, a conference on "The Languages of Criticism and the Sciences of Man" at Johns Hopkins in 1966 was considered the introduction of poststructuralism into the United States; Jacques Derrida and Paul De Man met for the first time, and there was a stellar cast of French literary experts and continental philosophers, including Derrida, Roland Barthes, Jean Hyppolite, and Jacques Lacan. The conference confirmed an overlapping archive that was developing between linguistic anthropology and literary cultural studies, consisting of Ferdinand de Saussure, Gottlob Frege, Charles Sanders Peirce,

John Austin, Nikolas Trubetzkoy, Roman Jakobson, and Emile Benveniste. Benveniste could be said to be the French forefather of both structuralism and the linguistic turn: he nominated Levi-Strauss for the Collège de France; Roland Barthes took his seminars; and he was a major influence upon Derrida, Pierre Bourdieu, Giles Deleuze, Michel Foucault, Jacques Lacan, and Jean-Pierre Vernant.

The interest in Austin's speech act inspired Jürgen Habermas to offer a "universal pragmatics" that was seen as opposed to Derrida's deconstructionism. Part of Habermas's revision of Kant replaced the "mind" with acts of communication (i.e., "speech acts") that he said presupposed a "communicational rationality" necessary for any mutual understanding. With the fall of the Soviet Union in 1989, there was a revival of interest in Habermas's habilitation thesis, *The Structural Transformation of the Public Sphere* (1989). Along with Benedict Anderson's *Imagined Community*, Habermas's book moved the linguistic turn to tackle national subjectivities by novels, newspapers, and new forms of public institutions such as coffee houses and salons.

The linguistic turn affected Postone, Silverstein, and Berlant differently. Postone was trained at the University of Frankfurt under Irving Fetscher, an expert on Hegel and Marx, and wrote *Labor, Time, and Social Domination* when he came to Chicago to the Center for Psychosocial Studies in 1983. He had a complicated relation to Jürgen Habermas, who was professor at the University of Frankfurt and became the German foil to Derrida. However, he considered Habermas's "universal pragmatics" to be "too linguistic" and offered instead an "immanent" critique that focused on the sociohistorical specificity of the concepts that explain contemporary capitalism.

Silverstein was trained under Roman Jakobson at Harvard at the height of the linguistic turn (the sixties) and was an intermediary between European structural linguistics and the research tradition that focused on Native American languages and included Franz Boas, Edward Sapir, and Benjamin Lee Whorf. Berlant was trained at Cornell in the early eighties; along with Yale, it was the center of literary cultural studies and deconstructionism. Cornell's comparative literature department was founded by Paul De Man, and one of its first students was Gayatri Spivak. One of Berlant's teachers at Cornell was Benedict Anderson, who in *Imagined Communities* raised the question that she would try to answer in *Cruel Optimism*: How did narration and print capitalism create new forms of social affect and identity such as patriotism and nationalism?

The Center for Psychosocial Studies

In the late eighties and nineties, Berlant, Postone, and Silverstein were project directors for the Center for Psychosocial Studies. They began a series of "Center forums" that looked at the "internationalization of culture and communication." The "social theory group," of which Postone and Tom McCarthy were codirectors, had received a prepublication copy of the English translation of Jürgen Habermas's *The Structural Transformation of the Public Sphere* and had begun intellectual exchanges with Charles Taylor and Pierre Bourdieu. In 1988, the Center for Psychosocial Studies set up a corresponding center at the Beijing Foreign Studies University whose courses featured a prepublication version of Taylor's *Sources of the Self*. Interest in civil society and the public sphere skyrocketed in 1989, which saw the downfall of the Soviet Union, the Tiananmen Square demonstrations and crackdown, and the first BJP Parliamentary election win in India. Through a variety of grants, the center was able to invite in residence intellectuals, writers, and academics from Russia, India, Europe, Hong Kong, Taiwan, and intellectual refugees from mainland China. The revised edition of Anderson's *Imagined Communities: Reflections on the Origin and Spread of Nationalism* (1991) appeared and joined *The Structural Transformation of the Public Sphere: An Inquiry into a Category of Bourgeois Society* and *Sources of the Self: The Making of Modern Identity* as theoretical reference points for center discussions. The result was a flurry of publications in which Berlant, Postone, and Silverstein were involved.

Postone wrote *Labor, Time, and Social Domination* when he arrived in 1983 and published it a decade later. In 1992, Craig Calhoun's edited volume *Habermas and the Public Sphere* appeared; Calhoun, Edward LiPuma, and Moishe Postone, working with Bourdieu, edited *Bourdieu: Critical Perspectives* in 1993. At the same time, the linguistics group under Silverstein and Greg Urban, with the assistance of Elizabeth Mertz, Richard Parmentier, and John Lucy, published *Semiotic Mediation* (1985), *Reflexive Language* (1993), and *The Natural Histories of Discourse* (1996). In 1992, Lauren Berlant and Michael Warner published "Critical Multiculturalism"–based upon conversations among international participants at the center forums that after 1989 focused on strengthening the public sphere–in *Critical Inquiry*. The linguistic turn had became public and global. In retrospect, the optimism in the public sphere and civil society rose as ways of regulating the excesses of global capitalism proved disappointing, perhaps an example of Berlant's "cruel optimism." The rise and fall of neoliberal capitalism, especially the crash of derivative finance in the Great Recession of 2007–2009 and the spread of new authoritarianisms, began a new era of volatility, for which traditional directional explanations seemed to fall short.

In 2017, a special issue of the literary journal *Representations* edited by Michael Lucey and Thomas McEnaney tried to introduce the work of linguistic anthropologists (especially Michael Silverstein) to literary cultural studies. The editors attempted to revise and revive the linguistic turn as relevant to the political critique of contemporary culture with these prescient words:

> [There is] a consensus that appears to have emerged in certain circles lately that traditional hermeneutic reading practices, especially "the hermeneutics of suspicion" and "symptomatic reading" no longer seem capable of carrying the political and ethical burden placed on them by earlier generations of Marxist, psychoanalytic, and new historicist critics. (Lucey and McEnaney 2017, 5)

Yet Berlant, Postone, and Silverstein later turned to critiques of neoliberalism, their ideas interlocking around issues of time and subjectivity in ways that might form the basis for a cross-disciplinary re-evaluation. A revived metapragmatic linguistic turn could unite Marxist and affect theories to criticize contemporary capitalism.

2
Benedict Anderson: Formulating the Question

In 1989, with the fall of the Soviet Union, progressive intellectuals thought that strengthening civil society and the public sphere would allow nations to control the spread of global capitalism. At that time, derivatives became the leading edge of finance capitalism; President Clinton deregulating them in 2000 unleashed a financial expansion until the Great Recession of 2007–2009. Most of *Cruel Optimism* was written during that expansion of neoliberal capitalism, which Berlant portrayed as a treadmill where people pursued neoliberal expectations but undermined their daily lives; her argument was influenced by Postone's insight about relative surplus value, in which the desire for material wealth undermines the value of labor. This new social affect, cruel optimism, was nurtured by a new phase of capitalism, the expansion of finance, and remains historically relevant through the rhetorical volatility of the present era driven by the new media. Although the GDP of the United States increased (mostly through finance and technology), the unequal distribution of wealth, the rise in infant mortality, and the increasing sense of volatility and risk indicated the downsides of neoliberal economic growth.

The template for *Cruel Optimism* was Anderson's *Imagined Communities: Reflections on the Origin and Spread of Nationalism*, which begins with the Tomb of the Unknown Soldier and asks how we created a notion of "we, the people" such that we would die for people we in principle as citizens might never know. How could we feel so strongly for people who weren't relatives or friends? Berlant raised a similar question: How did the new social affect of cruel optimism arise from the tropes and genres of neoliberal capitalism?

Anderson imaginatively expanded that discourse to the global rise of nationalism; he saw new national subjectivities as coming from the circulation of novels and newspapers, which would often be written in future national languages for audiences aware that they were reading about people like them who might never know or meet each other. Realistic third-person narration allowed the reader to occupy the place of an omniscient narrator (the view from nowhere) who simultaneously saw many independent plotlines unfolding, a microcosm of the imagined community of nationalism. The perspective of the omniscient narrator of novels and newspapers was analogous to a citizen surveying his fellow citizens' behavior in a nation-state. His famous example was taken from the Philippine nationalist writer Jose Rizal's *Noli Me Tangere*:

> Towards the end of October, Don Santiago de los Santos, popularly known as Capitan Tiago, was giving a dinner party. Although, contrary to his usual practice, he had announced it only that afternoon, it was already the subject of every conversation in Binondo, in other quarters of the city, and even in [the walled inner city of] Intramuros. In those days Capitan Tiago had the reputation of a lavish host. It was known that his house, like his country, closed its doors to nothing, except to commerce and to any new or daring idea.
>
> So the news coursed like an electric shock through the community of parasites, spongers, and gatecrashers whom God, in His infinite goodness, created, and so tenderly multiplies in Manila. Some hunted polish for their boots, others looked for

> collar-buttons and cravats. But one and all were preoccupied with the problem of how to greet their host with the familiarity required to create the appearance of long-standing friendship, or, if need be, to excuse themselves for not having arrived earlier. (Anderson 1991, 26–27)

Anderson remarked "that right from the start the image (wholly new to Filipino writing) of a dinner-party being discussed by hundreds of unnamed people, who do not know each other, in quite different parts of Manila, in a particular month of a particular decade, immediately conjures up the imagined community" (27); the third-person omniscient narrator became the "objective" perspective of these social imaginaries, including the nation-state, the public sphere, and the market, with each presupposing a distinct social affect: patriotism, freedom, and risk, respectively.

At the same time, novels and newspapers were commodities circulating in the "homogenous, empty time" of print capitalism. Realistic narration created an imagined community of strangers that produced new affects and emotions such as patriotism, which had an unspecified relation with the abstract time of capitalism. Anderson never specified the relationship between that time and narration, which coordinated the temporalities of a narrating event with those of the events narrated. How did narration produce the new, stranger mediated affects that new forms of national subjectivity demanded? How did cultural artifacts such as novels and newspapers produce the complex affective structures of late capitalism?

Anderson argued in *Imagined Communities* that nationalism is a combination of print capitalism, time, narration, and subjectivity. Postone addressed the problem of time and capitalism; an innovation-based capitalism was a dialectic between abstract and concrete labor times, with the former denominated in Newtonian absolute time. He narrowed the gap between abstract theoretical explanations of capitalism and the historical present by insisting that an immanent critique didn't employ outside transhistorical concepts but historically specific cultural concepts "internal" to the society; transhistorical concepts were abstracted from local contexts and placed in cross-disciplinary contexts, while historically specific concepts were like a culturally sensitive ethnography. Postone's "treadmill effect," set up by a linguistically mediated dialectic between abstract and concrete labor times, was the economic foundation in neoliberal capitalism for cruel optimism. Like her colleague Sianne Ngai's notion of the gimmick, innovations were "labor-saving tricks" that "strained efforts to get our attention" (Ngai 2020, 1). Berlant's treadmill structure of relative surplus value had a bivalent affective structure: whereas in an innovation-driven capitalism the pursuit of material wealth undermined the value of the labor needed to produce it, in cruel optimism the dreams of living a good life were people's aspirations at the same time hopes of gaining material wealth were fading away.

The dreams of prosperity decreased job security but increased risk and uncertainty. As contemporary capitalism increased material wealth by innovation, it undermined the value of labor so that as more people competed for more material wealth, job insecurity grew. Even as we thought we were succeeding, we were undercutting ourselves with cruel optimism.

However, Postone, by focusing on social science concepts like value, didn't give a historical account of how linguistic or rhetorical forms changed in the evolution of the European notion of time. Mathematical time, which is reversible, was opposed to duration or indexical time that flows from future to present to past. Newton and Einstein both said that our contemporary notion of time was contradictory. Silverstein gave an account of the contradiction of abstract and concrete times by examining our fashion of speaking about time. He argued that mathematical time as a "formless substance" came from the count-mass system of European languages and duration and the "flow of time" came from verbal tense.

It turned out that our fashion of speaking about time was a combination of the extensional absolute Newtonian time and indexical time given by linguistic tense, held together by the Standard Average European (SAE) count-mass system exemplified in measure phrases such as "two hours of time." Temporal measure units took whatever type of time was referred to by the head noun *time* and calibrated that with physical movements (flows of water, harmonic oscillations, or even radioactive decay) so that the notion of time in the head noun was instantiated in empirical reality. However, Silverstein never noticed that mathematical time and duration were the basis for Marx's distinction between abstract and concrete labor times. Abstract labor time was denominated in units of absolute time, and concrete labor time was a function of events and shifted with every productive context.

Postone and Silverstein each omitted what was important to the other; together they would fill the gap between Marx's concept of value and Berlant's historical present. Postone connected value to the contradiction between abstract and concrete labor times, whereas Silverstein clarified the linguistic roots of the same opposition between mathematical time and duration. Anderson said nationalism moved in the "homogenous, empty time," and abstract time was one of the dimensions of value. The contrast between mathematical and indexical times was also behind the continuum of rhetorical forms from which Berlant chose apostrophe and free indirect style to describe the creative destruction of cruel optimism.

But how do rhetorical genres make the connection with the structure of time that underlies value and capital? Berlant chose an article by Benveniste on apostrophe and another article by Jakobson on free indirect style to better understand the rhetorical "indirection" of cruel optimism. They both used the third-person pronoun, which according to Benveniste was an abstraction from the speaker and addressee and a "nonperson" to the ongoing speech act. It fitted third-person omniscient narration, which was the "view from nowhere," and the regimentation of third-person indirect discourse was crucial for the definition of mathematical time and also the fetish (value or abstract labor time was an abstraction from two exchangers like *I* and *you*).

Silverstein extended Jakobson and Benveniste to create a continuum of rhetorical forms that ranges from grammatical analogies to the rhetorical and poetic uses of language. This would be the rhetorical foundation for the "linguistic community," which contained all the competing rhetorical genres and was the linguistic mediation for new social affects. Instead of the monological nature of Anderson's "we, the people" (realistic narration) or Habermas's public sphere (universal pragmatics), the linguistic community was the sociohistorical interaction of all rhetorical genres. However, omniscient narration was the third-person perspective that one had to occupy to understand the stranger-mediated imagined communities of nationalism, the public sphere, and the market. Anderson described how the reading audiences of novels and newspapers could imagine other people like them reading the same novels in the same language and have similar responses, creating the common sensibility of nationalism. The next section describes how an immanent critique narrowed the gap between value and the historical present and how the fetish translated the dynamics of value into the tropes and genres that created social affects such as patriotism and cruel optimism.

3
Moishe Postone

Postone was the son of an orthodox rabbi who had survived the concentration camps. I joked with him once that his interpretation of volume I of *Capital* was like his father's reverent attitude to the Talmud; Postone replied that the Talmud wasn't an immanent critique. He was educated at the University of Chicago and the University of Frankfurt and became one of the leaders of Wertkritik ("value criticism"), which has become popular in Europe, especially Germany, France, and Italy.

In Germany, he developed an interpretation of Marx as an immanent critique, in contrast with the more transhistorically inclined Marxists in the United States, such as David Harvey. As Marx said in his second preface to volume I, he was a "pupil of that mighty thinker [Hegel], and even here and there, in the chapter on value, coquetted with the modes of expression peculiar to him" (Marx 1977, 14). He thought of Hegel's immanent critique as "standing on its head." Instead of the absolute concept unfolding itself into reality, Marx found a performative subject in surplus value or capital, which in positing itself created itself; Hegel's example of the absolute concept was the pronoun *I*. Postone maintained that in writing volume I (the only volume edited by Marx himself), especially in the section on value, Marx shifted from a transhistorical analysis of capitalism to a sociohistorically specific one.

An Immanent Critique

An immanent critique employed concepts from the object analyzed rather than imposing external transhistorical categories: "they are, as it were, categories of a critical ethnography of capitalist society undertaken from within" (Postone 1993, 18). By replacing transhistorical explanatory concepts with temporally sensitive cultural categories, Postone addressed Berlant's temporal gap between theoretical explanatory concepts and the historical present. It was internal to late capitalism that a temporal dialectic between abstract and concrete labor times appeared in relative surplus value. But an immanent critique was not simply a cross-culturally sensitive ethnography. Instead, a "Marxian analysis claims to be dialectical because it shows its object to be so" (Postone 1993,142).

Postone interpreted late Marx in terms of the sociohistorically specific mediation of labor, particularly abstract labor time as a general social mediation; he insisted that the structure of value produced the very forms of transhistorical analysis applied to ourselves and other societies. He criticized Harvey and other traditional Marxists for using transhistorical rather than historically contextualized categories. The premise of Wertkritik was that an immanent critique did not use a transhistorical or universal conception of labor; the goal of "revolution" would be to overturn the domination of abstract labor time rather than assume the perspective of labor or the working class.

Postone's evidence for this transition from transhistorical analysis to immanent critique was the changes made in the *Grundrisse* to *Contributions to the Critique of Political Economy* and finally volume I of *Capital*. The *Grundrisse* didn't include accounts of value and fetishism and *Contributions to the Critique of Political Economy* didn't include the simple form of value, which had two "peculiarities" that to Postone were the beginnings of fetishism. Volume I opened with a sociohistorically specific account of capitalism and then unfolded commodity exchange and the creation of surplus value; starting with the elementary form of exchange, the money dialectic, and absolute surplus value, it finished with relative surplus value.

The Fetish

Along the way, Marx also pointed out that the roots of fetishism/reification were already present in the simple form of value; when money became a general mediation for value (abstract labor time), then fetishism became a general property of society—value as abstract labor time became a general social mediation because most things were produced for money-mediated exchange. While the fetish was immanent in the simple form of value, it formed a totality mediated by value only when most things were produced for exchange among independent agents. If, following Postone's reasoning, fetishism was already immanent in the simple form of value, then the money fetish was a particular fetishism associated with the money form, and other fetishes were associated with absolute and relative surplus value. However, if the money fetish, in which the "definite social relation between men assumes the fantastic form of a relation between things," was extended to the financial neoliberalism of cruel optimism, then the fetish moved from treating people as commodities ("pricing" their preferences and values) to treating people as "human capital"[1] (portfolios of assets that maximized return but minimized risk).

The fetish form revealed the surface form of the temporal dialectic that drove both the money form and capital. In the money fetish, money indexed abstract labor time, i.e., value, but was also a commodity produced in socially and historically specific ways. The fetish was the surface form of the interaction between abstract and concrete labor time. In financial neoliberalism, this became a temporal dialectic between abstract and concrete labor time represented by Postone's famous treadmill; by ascribing affective value to the expectations of wealth and success raised by the fetishized forms of relative surplus value, we did not see that our attachments undermined our lives in the present. The negative effects of an innovation-based capitalism were not external effects of innovation but intrinsic to the creative destruction of relative surplus value itself.

The fetish was the basis for the transhistorical categories of classical economics; it treated the relationships between people as commodities with prices and then generalized that perspective. As Marx said, this was how social relationships appeared in capitalism when everything was produced for money-mediated exchange (when value, mediated by money, generates a social totality), but it is actually a partial view of a dialectical relationship between abstract and concrete labor time, which was ultimately realized in the treadmill effect of relative surplus value. Classical economists took a partial and transhistorical perspective on what was ultimately a dialectical process; human capital was the neoliberal version of the fetish because people didn't see labor underneath capital. For example, the derivative boom fed the growth of neoliberalism with more wealth, but the people involved didn't realize they were also increasing the volatility and risk of capital.

Value: The Dialectic of Time and the Treadmill of Relative Surplus Value

Postone argued that the temporal dialectic of abstract and concrete labor time realized its immanent form in relative surplus value. Abstract labor time was virtual in the simple form of value; it represented the identity expressed by *twenty yards of linen = one suit*. Linen and a suit were quite different, so Marx read the identity statement as representing what linen and suits had in common, which was only that they were both the products of concrete labor;

the relative form, twenty yards of linen, expressed its value in the equivalent form, one suit. Because these labors were qualitatively different, they could only be equivalent at an abstract level, i.e., the absolute time needed to produce them.

In the simple form of value, the mediation of abstract labor time was local and not a general mediation of totality. In the expanded form, the identity was shared by several commodities, and in the money form, everything was exchanged for quantities of everything else and money became the medium of exchange. Value became a general social mediation of the totality of exchanges; when most things were produced to exchange, the social totality had a general abstract mediation, i.e., abstract labor time. Value in the form of abstract labor time was denominated in measure units of absolute Newtonian time: seconds, minutes, hours, and days. Time was "homogenous and empty" and infinitely divisible, and each unit measured the same "amount" so that sixty minutes was substituted for an hour and twenty-four hours for a day; these constant hours were intersubstitutable like the numbers $3 + 3$, $8 - 2$, $\sqrt{36}$, and 6. Absolute Newtonian time was extensional and became the framework in which all events took place—they could be dated in calendar time.

"Abstract time," on the other hand, by which I mean uniform, continuous, homogeneous, "empty" time, is independent of events. The conception of abstract time, which became increasingly dominant in Western Europe between the fourteenth and seventeenth centuries, was expressed most emphatically in Newton' s formulation of "absolute, true and mathematical time [which] flows equably without relation to anything external." Abstract time is an independent variable; it constitutes an independent framework within which motion, events, and action occur. Such time is divisible into equal, constant, nonqualitative units. (Postone 1993, 202)

According to Postone, absolute time developed only in modern Western Europe, and concrete time was the time determined by events. The infinitely divisible quality of Newtonian absolute time derived from the notion of an infinitesimal that played such an important role in Newton's development of calculus.

Postone considered capitalism as a new form of social domination created by abstract time, and the global spread of capitalism as indexed by the circulation of mechanical clocks and the Gregorian calendar. This supplanted local "concrete" times, which were associated with "agrarian, natural rhythms of life and work that depended on the cycles of the seasons and of day and night." Since the measure unit *hour* varied with the amount of daylight, concrete hours were variable and thus not extensional;

concrete time was a function of events: “A relationship exists between the measure of time and the sort of time involved. The fact that the time unit is not constant, but itself varies, indicates that this form of time is a dependent variable, a function of events, occurrences, or actions” (Postone 1993, 202).

Concrete time was calibrated to indexical events and was also logically nonextensional–speech indexicals such as deictics or tense, for example, shifted their references with the speech event. For example, the present tense was dependent upon the event of speaking, with which it was simultaneous; the past and future tenses were similarly dependent. The past tense referred to a time before it and the future tense to a time after it. The contradiction of mathematical and indexical time was reflected in the dialectic of abstract and concrete times of relative surplus value, which described the creative destruction of technological innovation and produced the treadmill effect of capitalism.

In retrospect, the opposition between objectivity and subjectivity has been the split between scientific causality and creative freedom, perhaps best exemplified in Kant’s aesthetics (Kant absorbed Newton’s positions on time, space, and causality). Of course, the Western history of time didn’t have constant hours until the invention of mechanical clocks, and Postone had a section in *Time, Labor, and*

Social Domination on the importation of the Western calendar and clocks into China, which emphasized a different approach to the "objective" and the "subjective." The most accurate clock in the world for over five hundred years was a water clock in China, but it was used only for astronomical observations and not exported into business and commerce, which used the solunar calendar with variable hours. In the latter half of the nineteenth century, China, Korea, and Japan became involved in an arms race and imported engineering and Western manufacturing because they needed to produce machine guns and long-range artillery. East Asia came under the domination of abstract labor time and the production of relative surplus value in the form of technological innovation.

However, relative surplus value also produced a treadmill effect. The value of commodities was the amount of abstract labor time needed to produce them, denominated in units of Newtonian absolute time such as infinitely divisible constant hours. However, the efficiency or productivity of labor depended upon concrete time, the qualitative sociohistorically specific forms needed to produce any particular commodity. A technological innovation made labor more efficient in that more commodities (material wealth) were produced per unit of abstract time. For example, a hundred pounds of cotton would take two hours to produce; the innovation might produce the same amount in an hour, decreasing the value of the hundred pounds of cotton by half.

However, an increase in labor productivity had an inverse effect on value, as the abstract labor time needed to produce a commodity decreased. If the innovation and what it replaced sold at the same price, then the capitalist pocketed the difference as "relative surplus value" until the innovation spread and became the new standard; the new labor productivity of the innovation normalized ("the socially necessary labor time"), creating a dialectic between value (abstract labor time) and material wealth (the mass of commodities and concrete labor time), whose contradiction deepened as "historical time" proceeded.

In Marxist theory, the role of finance was controversial ("fictitious"), as it created monetary wealth out of proportion to the labor time required and only accentuated the contradiction between value and wealth. Postone gave this contradiction a colorful name: *the treadmill*. Capitalism was driven to produce surplus value, increasing the productivity of labor and material wealth even as it devalued labor. The treadmill effect was a form of abstract domination: even though value was denominated in abstract time, capitalism was driven by the innovation at the heart of relative surplus value to increase the productivity of labor, which produced more wealth but at the same time devalued labor time.

This worked at the level of individual innovation but had a cumulative collective effect. In a society driven by the pursuit of relative surplus value, innovation occurred across commodities and sectors, decreasing value and increasing material wealth if demand kept up apace. Since workers consumed commodities in order to reproduce themselves, the socially necessary labor time needed to reproduce the worker decreased and the rate of profit fell. What is good for capitalist societies on the surface (more material wealth) is bad for them at an existential level.

The treadmill effect was set up by a dialectic between abstract and concrete time that would produce *historical time*, which determined the sociohistorical level of labor productivity.

The dialectic of the two dimensions of labor in capitalism, then, can also be understood temporally, as a dialectic of two forms of time. As we have seen, the dialectic of concrete and abstract labor results in an intrinsic dynamic characterized by a peculiar treadmill pattern. Because each new level of productivity is redetermined as a new base level, this dynamic tends to become ongoing and is marked by ever-increasing levels of productivity. Considered temporally, this intrinsic dynamic of capital, with its treadmill pattern, entails an ongoing directional movement of time, a "flow of history." In other words, the mode of concrete time we are examining can be considered historical time, as constituted in capitalist society. (Postone 1993, 293)

Historical time was the result of the dialectic of two times. Abstract time was the absolute time of Newton, which was presupposed by classical physics and engineering. In addition to being an independent variable with respect to events, it was an infinitely divisible timeline along which any event could be dated, acting as the framework for all events. Concrete time was calibrated by events—it acted as a dependent variable. In addition, constant hours were a prerequisite for Newton's absolute time. Postone described medieval Europe and traditional China as running under solunar calendars in which hours varied with the amount of daylight and therefore were shorter in the winter than in the summer. Constant and uniform measure units were required for Newtonian physics and classical engineering.

Sianne Ngai saw Postone's treadmill effect as a dynamic motivation for affective changes in capitalism, especially the nature of the gimmick as arousing ambivalent feelings that were similar to cruel optimism. However, the treadmill effect was a product of an immanent critique—it used cultural categories of time (mathematical and indexical times) to describe a structure feeling that was also ambivalent—what we desired undermined us. Retrospectively, cruel optimism had a treadmill structure—something wanted (more material wealth) undermined everyday reality (the value of labor).

Postone prepared for Anderson and Berlant's translation of value into narration by analyzing the fetish. It was immanent in the simple form of value:

> Whence, then, arises the enigmatic character of the product of labour, as soon as it assumes the form of a commodity? Clearly, it arises from this form itself. The equality of the kinds of human labour takes on a physical form in the equal objectivity of the products of labour as values; the measure of the expenditure of human labour by its duration takes on the form of the magnitude of the products of labour; and finally the relationships between the producers, within which the social characteristics of their labours are manifested, take on the form of a social relation between the products of labour. (Marx 1977, 164)

The exchange of commodities made an equivalence between twenty yards of linen and one suit such that they were exchanged: *twenty yards of linen = one suit*. Marx read this as a statement that since linen and suit had no equivalence in use value, something beyond the two commodities extended to an abstract quality that they both shared, the amount of labor time necessary to produce them. This third, immanent in these two commodities as products of labor and exchanged, didn't exist in itself but was a component he compared to propyl formate and butyric acid, which had the same chemical formula $C_4H_8O_2$ but very distinct properties: the former was used for perfumes and the latter was an ingredient in human flatulence.

The same argument was given in Frege's "Sense and Reference," that an identity statement "*a* = *a*" was "a priori" but "*a* = *b* often contained very valuable extension of our knowledge" (Frege 1962, 56). $C_4H_8O_2$ was the referent and propyl formate and butyric acid were the senses; *twenty yards of linen* = *twenty yards of linen* was not informative and "not an expression of value" (Marx 1977, 140). The secret of value was in the equivalence *twenty yards of linen* = *one suit*, in which the relative and equivalent forms had an identity in a nonpresent third that wasn't shared by face-to-face exchangers. This resembled Frege's sense and reference distinction, where he said an identity statement like "*a* = *b*" was the epistemological route to new knowledge. The "third person" was not present at the moment of speaking, and third-person narration, the "view from nowhere," was the overlap between fetishism and narration and translated the fetish into narration and the dialectic of time that was instantiated in relative surplus value.

However, the next section describes how Frege used indirect discourse to make his distinction between sense and reference. Indirect discourse, the standard way of representing speech, was the crucial component of the continuum of rhetorical and narrative forms that Silverstein discovered and Berlant used to create her flow model of subjectivity. Because Frege was a logician, he focused on the referential and semantic functions of language. Jakobson extended those functions to rhetoric and the poetic uses of language, and Silverstein expanded them to include ritual discourse. From Marx's discussion of exchange, one could see the fetish and rhetoric as immanent in the simple form of commodity, realized as a temporal dialectic in relative surplus value and forming the treadmill structure of cruel optimism.

4
The Linguistic Turn

The beginning of the linguistic turn in structuralism insisted on the autonomy of language and logic. Saussure distinguished the structure of language (*langue* or grammar) from indexicality (*parole*), which was tied to the moment of speaking. He fought for the autonomy of *langue* but cut off *langue* from pragmatics and indexicality. For Frege, the sentence had a truth value that made it analyzable by quantificational logic but didn't include the rhetorical or poetic uses of language. Ambiguity wasn't suitable for mathematics and logic and had to be ruled out. Analytic philosophers would extend Frege's logical insights to indexicality (pragmatics) and modality (possibility/necessity).

Saussure's definition of a linguistic sign was the correspondence between differences in sound (signifiers) and differences in meaning (signifieds or semantic concepts), and had two dimensions: an axis of selection (paradigmatic) and an axis of combination (syntagmatic). For example, the paradigmatic axis was the choice of b, m, c, and s in front of the syntagmatic combination of _-a-t, differentiating the words *bat*, *mat*, *cat*, and *sat*. The famous Saussurean proportion was an analogy:

At the end of nouns in English,
Ø : -s :: singular : plural

However, Saussure maintained a strong distinction between *langue* and *parole*. *Langue* was in the realm of grammar and nonindexicality and *parole* included indexicality or pragmatics. Since the sentence was in *parole*, he didn't see rhetoric and poetry as belonging to *langue*.

Frege tried to translate natural language into logical form for mathematics where ambiguity was ruled out and also didn't consider the rhetorical or poetic uses of languages. However, Saussure and Frege disagreed about the role of the sentence. For Saussure, the sentence was in parole and not subject to grammatical analysis; however, for Frege the sentence had a truth value and was subject to logical analysis. After Frege logicians would use intensional logics to analyze indexicality. Silverstein would take a different path, the semiotic route that led to ritual and social context. Metapragmatics are the metalinguistic descriptions of the different pragmatics of speech acts beyond constatives. These different speech acts are responsible for the "performative" constructions of tropes and genres into new social imaginaries such as the market, originally built from promises and contracts.

Frege noticed that mathematics and science allowed the intersubstitution of *co-referential* terms *salve veritate* or without change of truth value in the expressions of which they were part; these contexts became known as *extensional*. For example, definitions were considered to be coreferential and extensional: *eye doctor* and *opthamologist* picked out the same people and 2^2, 4, and 2 + 2 referred to the same number. Contexts like indexicality, subjectivity, and modality where reference shifted were *intensional*. *This, that, here, there*, and verbal tense shifted their references with a new speech event. If *8 = the number of planets*, it was *possible that 8 = the number of planets* was true but *necessary that 8 = the number of planets* was in turn false; modality was intensional. Intensional contexts were where substitution of coreferential terms failed.

Frege focused on epistemological contexts such as the sentence *Galileo believes that the morning star is the evening star*, which under one interpretation was false if Galileo didn't know that *morning star* and *evening star* referred to the same planet, in this case, the planet Venus. If the sense of the morning star was the brightest star in the morning sky and the sense of the evening star was the brightest star in the evening sky, the sentence *Galileo doesn't believe that the morning star = the evening star* was true because in epistemic contexts coreferential terms referred to their senses and not to their referents.

Verbs of thinking, feeling, and speaking that contained subordinating conjunctions (*that* in English, *dass* in German, or *si* and *que* in French or Italian) and were followed by nominal complements (*he believes that...*, *he is angry that...*, *he promises that...*) were intensional contexts in which coreferential terms shifted references, but mathematics and science were instead extensional, where coreferential terms could be substituted salve veritate. Indexicality, subjectivity (verbs of thinking, feeling, and speaking), and modality (possibility and necessity) were contexts where reference shifted and were intensional.

The Road Not Taken

Building upon Frege's founding of mathematical logic, Alfred Tarski started the logical (semantic) approach to truth in the 1930s, trying to give a logical definition robust enough for mathematics. He started with the liar's paradox, *This sentence is false*, which if true was false or if false was true, leading to a contradiction. Tarski saw that a definition of truth had to be in a metalanguage that referred to the object language; his famous example was *"Snow is white" if and only if snow is white*, where the metalanguage was in quotes and referred to the object language, not quoted. The hierarchy of metalanguages and object languages was unlimited. Jakobson saw the self-referential uses of language as metalanguage and contrasted the poetic function (which focused on the message) to the metalingual function (which focused on the code). Every metalanguage had its own pragmatics, which determined its use; for reference, the use would be "glossing" or giving definitions. A description of that pragmatics would be "metapragmatics," and every level of metasemantics had its own pragmatics and metapragmatics.

Jakobson absorbed Tarski's work on truth, and it became the foundation for his notion of metalanguage, which he extended to the poetic uses of language. Jakobson had immersed himself in the world of poetry in Moscow before World War I and was motivated by his fellow poets to become a linguist. His interest in poetry never faded; he once said, "I privately believe that the poetic incompetence of some bigoted linguists has been mistaken for an inadequacy of the linguistic science itself" (Jakobson 1960, 377). Although he accepted that linguistics had to be a science, he wanted it to be "a science that studies the life of sign within society" (Sperber 2008, 309) and all forms of communication and culture.

In one version of "Closing Statement: Linguistics and Poetics," he referenced Tarski in the original Polish! Jakobson, in his articles on aphasia, talked about metalanguage and identified the tropes of metaphor and metonymy with similarity and contiguity; he also identified the paradigmatic axis with selection (synonyms could be selected in the same paradigmatic slot) and the syntagmatic axis with combination, leading to the famous statement that the poetic function projected the axis of selection on the axis of combination:

> To answer this question we must recall the two basic modes of arrangement used in verbal behavior, *selection* and *combination*... The selection is produced on the base of equivalence, similarity and dissimilarity, synonymity and antonymity, while the combination, the build up of the sequence,

> is based on contiguity. *The poetic function projects the principle of equivalence from the axis of selection into the axis of combination.* (Jakobson 1960, 358)

His example was meter, which might repeat itself after some fixed number of metrical feet (for example, iambic pentameter consists of five metrical feet, each consisting of an unstressed and a stressed syllable). Meter made the audience focus on similarities across the syntagmatic unfolding of discourse; for example, end rhymes drew attention to the last words of these lines.

Whereas Jakobson's insights about metaphor and metonymy and the linguistic sign were very influential in literary studies, Tarski's writings about metalanguage did not have much impact because they were technical. One of the articles that Berlant selected as a theoretical framework for cruel optimism was a commentary by Barbara Johnson on Jakobson's work on metaphor and metonymy in her analysis of free indirect style in Zora Hurston; the other article used Benveniste to analyze the use of apostrophe in poems about abortion. Johnson was a graduate student of Paul De Man at Yale, so there was a line from Berlant to Johnson to De Man.

Paul De Man came as Carpenter lecturer to the University of Chicago in the spring of 1979; he taught his course on rhetoric from the manuscript of *Allegories of Reading*, which would appear in the fall of 1979. Silverstein wrote "Metaforces of Traditional Oratory" in 1980 and gave it at Chicago and Yale in the winter of 1981, but he and De Man never met. However, both were extending Jakobson's work on metalanguage to "metafigural functions" or "metapragmatics" and reached the same conclusion: rhetorical genres were defined by a continuum that ranged from the axis of selection (De Man's "rhetorization of grammar" or Tarski's "metasemantics") to the axis of combination (De Man's "grammatization of rhetoric" or Silverstein's "metapragmatics").

In 1973, De Man wrote an essay for *Diacritics*, "Semiology and Rhetoric," that was unabashed about how Jakobson influenced him on metaphor and metonymy. Less recognized was how much Tarski's article on truth and the liar's paradox influenced him on the nature of deconstructionism. In his articles on aphasia, Jakobson had caused a stir in the humanities by identifying the axis of selection (the paradigmatic axis) with metaphor and the axis of combination (the syntagmatic axis) with metonymy, indicating tropes as a constitutive part of the linguistic sign. In "Closing Statement: Linguistics and Poetics" (1987), Jakobson referenced Tarski on metalanguage.

"Semiology and Rhetoric" became the first chapter in *Allegories of Reading*, perhaps the most influential book in deconstructionist literary theory. De Man complained in this chapter that

> Barthes, Genette, Todorov, Greimas and their disciples all simplify and regress from Jakobson in letting grammar and rhetoric function in perfect continuity and in passing from grammatical to rhetorical structures without difficulty or interruption. Indeed, as the study of grammatical structures is refined in contemporary theories of generative, transformational and distributive grammar, the study of tropes and figures (which is how the term rhetoric is used throughout this paper, and not in the derived sense of comment or of eloquence or persuasion) becomes a mere extension of grammatical models, a particular subset of syntactical relations. (De Man 1979, 6)

He then said that rhetoric has to be concerned with "deflection," and Charles Sanders Peirce who, with Nietzche and Saussure, laid the philosophical foundation for modern semiology, stressed the distinction between grammar and rhetoric in his celebrated and suggestively unfathomable definition of the sign... the interpretation of the sign is not, for Peirce, a meaning but another sign; it is a reading, not a decodage, and this reading has, in its turn, to be interpreted into another sign, and so on *ad infinitum*. (De Man 1979, 8-9)

This was a reprise of Jakobson's criticism of Saussure's dyadic notion of the linguistic sign and the affirmation of the Peircean translation of a sign into another sign. "Semiology and Rhetoric" analyzed the *metafigural* functions of language, taken directly from Jakobson's writing on metalanguage.

Berlant also chose "deflection" or rhetorical "indirection" for the analysis of affect: "to understand cruel optimism, therefore, one must embark on an analysis of indirection ... I learned how to do this from reading Barbara Johnson on apostrophe and free indirect discourse" (Berlant 2011, 25). The articles that Berlant selected were based upon specific articles by Benveniste and Jakobson, who provided the linguistic tools to do "close readings" from a deconstructionist angle. She was invoking the rhetorical dimensions of the linguistic turn and asked how affect interacted with linguistic mediation and rhetoric. Berlant showed that these affective sensibilities influence everyday life but feed into the structure of contemporary capitalism. By focusing on rhetorical indirection, she uncovered a renewed political direction for the linguistic turn. The articles that Berlant chose were about how tropes and linguistic structure (especially Benveniste and Jakobson) interacted and also addressed contemporary cultural issues, like abortion and race ("Apostrophe, Animation, and Abortion" and "Metaphor, Metonym, Voice in *Their Eyes Were Watching God*").

"Indirection" or "deflection" were stand-ins for rhetoric. De Man's "metafigural functions" were based on Jakobson's "metalingual function"; Jakobson identified metaphor and metonymy with the paradigmatic and syntagmatic axes of the linguistic sign. The metafigural was also metapragmatic but talked about tropes. De Man's analysis of the metafigural started with the case where a syntagm had multiple rhetorical interpretations, which he called the "rhetorization of grammar." His example was the famous last line of Yeats's poem *Among School Children*: "How can we know the dancer from the dance?," which could be read as a literal or rhetorical question; either interpretation would be supported by the syntagmatic unfolding of the poem. By controlling the syntagmatic dimension, he could focus on the play of similarity and dissimilarity among alternates on the axis of selection. Since the two readings had similar backing throughout the whole poem, neither reading "can be given priority over the other since neither exist[s] in the other's absence." The reader seemed to end up "in a suspended ignorance" between interpretations.

The other metafigural function was the "grammatization of rhetoric," which described how tropes interacted in the syntagmatic unfolding of the text. His example, from Proust's *Swann's Way*, focused on the interplay between tropes as the syntagmatic axis was unfolding. The passage was about the superiority of metaphor over metonymy but "the assertion of the mastery of metaphor over metonymy owes its persuasive power to the use of metonymic structure," which applied Jakobson's words about metaphor and metonymy to an argument about freedom and creativity:

> By passing from a paradigmatic structure based on substitution, such as metaphor, to a syntagmatic structure based on contingent association such as metonymy, the mechanical, repetitive aspect of grammatical forms is shown to be operative in a passage that seemed at first sight to celebrate the self-willed and autonomous inventiveness of a subject ... Yet, our reading of the Proust passage shows that precisely when the highest claims are being made for the unifying power of metaphor, these very images rely in fact on the deceptive of semi-automatic grammatical patterns. (De Man 1979, 15)

Although the text asserted the superiority of metaphor over metonymy and rhetoric over grammar, it also showed how this assertion was deconstructed by the syntagmatic and metonymic structures of grammar. At first glance, the grammatization of rhetoric ended up in a "negative certainty," which would be an affirmation of deconstructive readings. De Man then followed his deconstruction of metaphor in Proust with perhaps his most controversial statement: that deconstructionism would become "the task of literary criticism in the following years" (De Man 1979, 17).

Few interpreters of De Man's statement recognized that it was meant to be ironical, not a prediction of things to become. De Man used the mutual influence of metaphor and metonym as the basis for criticizing overzealous and perhaps naive acolytes of deconstructionism who were convinced too early by a deconstructionist reading. The argument drew upon Tarski's work on defining truth, which Jakobson referenced in "Closing Statement: Linguistics and Poetics." After we had deconstructed the assertion that metaphor was superior to metonymy, he asked the further (metafigural) question "whether the rhetorical mode of the text in question is metaphor or metonymy" and determined "it is impossible to give an answer" because the narrator was a combination of a grammatical person (often the third person) and a rhetorical voice and was responsible for whatever was said or narrated. It was the metafigural counterpart to asking whether a sentence is true or false, a metasemantic question. The assertion of the superiority of metaphor was deconstructed by the metonymic structure of grammar, but that structure "has as its subject a voice whose relationship to this clause is again metaphorical" (De Man 1979, 18); the narrator who deconstructed metaphor by metonymy was itself a metaphor (had a voice). The result was not a simple assertion of the superiority of deconstructionism but an unending succession of readings that ended up in suspended ignorance—the rhetorical counterpart to the self-reflexivity of the liar's paradox. This led to the same suspended ignorance as the rhetorization of grammar and consisted of a never-ending succession of metalevels:

> We end up therefore, in the case of the rhetorical grammatization of semiology, just as in the grammatical rhetorization of illocutionary phrases, in the same state of suspended ignorance. Any question about the rhetorical mode of a literary text is always a rhetorical question which does not even know whether it is really questioning ... Literature as well as criticism—the difference between them being delusive—is condemned (or privileged) to be forever the most rigorous and, consequently, the most

> unreliable language in terms of which man names and transforms himself. (De Man 1979, 19)

The grammatization of rhetoric ended in the same suspended ignorance or indeterminacy as the rhetorization of grammar. Both metafigural functions involved directional interpretations (rhetorical/literal, metaphor/metonymy), but they "hedged" each other out, leaving in suspended ignorance to the next moment of interpretation, as the undecidability dynamically replicated through language.

Silverstein never met De Man at Chicago, and an opportunity for linguistic anthropology and literary cultural studies was lost. But in the mid-seventies, the linguistic turn was going through a "metalinguistic" revolution in which a major influence was Jakobson. De Man's rhetorization of grammar and the grammatization of rhetoric were metafigural functions that self-reflexively compared syntagms (metaphor) under different rhetorical interpretations and watched rhetorical tropes interact across the unfolding of discourse (metonymy). These two dimensions defined the continuum of rhetorical tropes from glossing (metaphor) to the poetic uses of language (metonymy) that Silverstein outlined in "Metaforces of Power in Traditional Oratory." Both implied that this continuum of rhetorical forms made up a linguistic community relevant to contemporary cultural analyses, especially in the case of nationalism (Anderson) and the public sphere (Habermas).

Often overlooked was that De Man raised a similar question to Tarski–whether asking if was a sentence was true or false required a recursion of metalanguages to answer. Was the sentence metaphorical or metonymic? Was it rhetorical? That led to a rhetorical paradox that rivaled the liar's paradox: each metalevel required a new metalanguage to express the very question: Was it rhetorical or nonrhetorical, true or false? Literary theorists did not build upon De Man's insight that the question was also undecidable and led to a similar series of metalevels. Silverstein implied that every metalevel has its own pragmatics, which could be referred to in a metalanguage that would have its own pragmatics, a potentially infinite recursion.

At the end of his life, De Man was working on a rhetorical interpretation of Marx's *German Ideology*; it made it possible that a revised linguistic turn would answer Berlant and Anderson's questions about print capitalism, narrative genres, and new social affects. Although in "Semiology and Rhetoric" he incorporated Jakobson's and Tarski's insights about metalanguage, he used them to discuss the undecidability of rhetoric, not to ask questions about the semiotic mediation of social action. *The German Ideology* was an early work (1845) and had the base and superstructure of early Marx but no accounts of value, surplus value, or fetishism. Berlant and Anderson's questions could not be formulated until Silverstein's work on metapragmatics, which saw the linguistic community as made up of competing and interacting rhetorical genres that semiotically mediate capitalism. How would a revised linguistic turn connect the abstract explanations of relative surplus value to the indexicality of the historical present? How did narrative genres make the dialectic of abstract and concrete labor times in relative surplus value create new social affects such as cruel optimism?

5
Metapragmatics

But what did "metapragmatics" look like? Silverstein extended Jakobson's work on metalanguage to a metapragmatic continuum of rhetorical and poetic forms ranging from grammatical analogy to the performativity of ritual discourse that makes up the linguistic community that mediates social action. The anthropological linguist Benjamin Lee Whorf maintained that the grammatical mediation of thought and behavior in Standard Average European (SAE) linguistic communities influenced basic assumptions in finance, accounting, history, and philosophy of the form/substance distinction. Silverstein extended Whorf's analysis of our fashion of speaking about time to the collective subjectivity of "we, the people" and nationalism.

This pamphlet will explore how the "fashions of speaking" interact and the social ramifications of this continuum by analyzing the grammatical analogies that make up the worldviews about time and subjectivity.

However, Whorf and Silverstein didn't explore the fundamental contradiction of our fashion of speaking about time that both Newton and Einstein pointed out, which was the source of C. P. Snow's remark that there were "two cultures" of the sciences and humanities. The fashion of speaking about time interacted with fashions of subjectivity that created new affects and emotions that also fed into the fundamental contradiction in capitalism. According to Marxists the temporal contradiction was based upon the relation between abstract labor time, which was extensional and mathematical, and concrete labor time, which was indexical, intensional, and a function of events.

Silverstein introduced the term "metapragmatics" into linguistic anthropology in 1976. The notion of "metalanguage" was hot, especially at the University of Chicago. Saul Kripke's lectures that formed *Naming and Necessity* (1980) were delivered in 1970 at Princeton and immediately catalyzed the development of intensional logics, which were then applied to language. He came out with his revision of Tarski, "Outline to a Theory of Truth," in 1975, and Donald Davidson, who adopted Tarski's semantic approach to truth and applied it to meaning, came to Chicago in 1976.

Metapragmatics: Saussure and Frege

Silverstein wrote two papers in 1976; the first was for a technical audience in linguistics, "Hierarchy of Features and Ergativity," and the other was for anthropologists, "Shifters, Linguistic Categories, and Cultural Description." The former didn't mention metapragmatics, but in an article in 1981 he explained that metapragmatics underlay the noun phrase hierarchy of features, which his 1976 article explored. The "Shifters" article was an extension of Jakobson's eponymous "Shifters, Verbal Categories, and the Russian Verb" and introduced the semiotics of Peirce into linguistic anthropology, after which he explicitly mentioned "metapragmatics." Unlike Saussure, who did not include pragmatics or indexicality in *langue* or grammar, he believed the noun phrase was a marking hierarchy between pragmatics and metapragmatics or indexicality or metaindexicality. In the analytic philosophy of language, there was a tradition that incorporated indexicality as reference shift. However, they saw the sentence as analyzable through quantificational logic, which meant it was self-referential and did not include the rhetorical or poetic uses of language.

Silverstein, who had the logician W. V. Quine and Jakobson as mentors, combined the Fregean and Saussurean traditions in a unique semiotic synthesis. When Jakobson came to the United States, he had switched from Husserl to the philosopher Charles Sanders Peirce for a semiotic interpretation of indexicality. Peirce, a codiscoverer of quantificational logic with Frege, was much esteemed by Quine; Silverstein adopted both logical and semiotic analyses of indexicality (shifters) from Peirce. Peirce saw the proposition as built up of different types of signs, including proper names as indices. Indices were tied to events, signaling a copresence with the sign and its object that shifted reference with every moment of speaking.

In the "Shifters" article, Silverstein introduced the Peircean trichotomy of signs of icons, indices, and symbols, and then analyzed indices as events. Since events transform parameters of the context and leave others unchanged, Silverstein divided indices into two dimensions: referential/nonreferential and presupposing/creative. Referential indices were deictics like *here* or *this*, which referred to some parameter of the moment of speaking; nonreferential indices, like honorifics, indexed status but didn't refer to it, like the difference between *tu* and *vous* in French. The presupposing and creative dimension referred to the indexical parameters they transformed or left unchanged.

Silverstein incorporated the extension/intension distinction in his "Three Faces of Function" (1987). He saw the referential function as nonindexical (what he called *referential function*$_2$) and extensional, which was a combination of Saussure's nonindexicality and Frege's logical analysis. Unlike intensional logicians, who extended extensional logic by adding another logical dimension (*possible worlds* analysis taken from Kripke's modal logic), he reserved *pragmatic function*$_2$ for indices and presupposed the event structure of speech acts. Because they were tied to events, linguistic indices had both referential/nonreferential and presupposing/creative dimensions. Unlike for Saussure and Frege, the linguistic sign was connected to events, which meant it mediated social action.

Silverstein then distinguished the goal-directed uses of language (speech acts) as *pragmatic function*$_1$, which tied the uses of language to grammar. Building upon Jakobson's discussion of metalanguage, he identified grammar with glossing, giving definitions, which fit into analytic philosophy's extension/intension distinction. Since grammar was given by glossing or making definitions (semantic equivalences) and definitions were intersubstitutable (e.g., *opthamologist* and *eye doctor*), this dimension was nonindexical (referential function$_2$); however, referential indices such as deictics had an intensional component that shifted their references, which was subject to an indexical dimension (pragmatic function$_2$). The noun phrase hierarchy was governed by "metapragmatic transparency," which was a metalinguistic relationship between indexicality and metaindexicality, which in turn determined case marking, nominative-ergative relationships, and coreference.

"The Hierarchy of Features" and "Shifters" Articles

Silverstein distinguished himself from other scholars in the seventies by eschewing both extensional and intensional logical analyses of grammar. Instead, in the "Shifters" article, he outlined a Peircean semiotic route to indexicality and insisted that it had to be analyzed as an event, with its presupposing and creative dimensions. This also meant that linguistic indexicality and speech events were a mediating factor in social action.

He added another perspective, Prague School marking theory, learned from Jakobson, one of the founders of the Prague School of Linguistics along with his close friend Nikolai Trubetzkoy. Neutralization was a concept crucial to marking theory. It was discovered by Trubetzkoy in his pathbreaking *Grundzüge der Phonologie*, which became a classic of the Prague School because it introduced marking theory and neutralization to structural linguistics. Extending the Saussurean semantic approach to phonology, Trubetzkoy and Jakobson analyzed the referential function in terms of marking theory in which the neutralization of phonemes (distinctive features) occurred in specific syntagms, such as the devoicing in final position in German. For example, the opposition between voiced and unvoiced features didn't appear in final position in nouns in German; *Rat* and *Rad* were neutralized and pronounced as *Rat* (unvoiced and unmarked). Neutralization also allowed for phonological ambiguity between words, which wasn't allowed in logical analyses; *Rat* and *Rad* were the same sound applied to two different words, and *man* was applied to two different semantic meanings.

Jakobson extended marking theory from phonology to semantics. A semantic example was *man*, which had two meanings: an unmarked meaning that meant human beings in general, distinct from *man* (male beings) as opposed to *woman* (female beings). Silverstein, translating neutralization and marking theory from phonology to semantics, gave a formal rule for the relationships between grammatical features in his "Hierarchy of Features and Ergativity" article:

> Let grammatical feature [F_i] code semantic property A. Then [+F_j] means 'A' while [-F_i] is interpreted as failure to specify A, i.e., [-F_i] means ~ 'A'. But residually,
>
> $$\sim \text{'A'} \Rightarrow \text{'}\sim\text{A'},$$
>
> i.e., [-F_i] *can be* interpreted as the negative of A. (Silverstein 1976a, 170)

Part of the social criticism of *man* as unmarked was that human beings were seen as having male characteristics, which was a projection from a grammatical analogy. If extended to grammatical categories, there was the possibility of ambiguity and grammatical analogy (*man* had two semantic meanings, human beings versus male persons as opposed to female persons)[2] as one word influenced the semantic meaning of the other. This was very different from logical analysis, where semantic ambiguity was to be avoided.

Figure 1 shows part of the noun phrase hierarchy, the application of Silverstein and Jakobson's rule for markedness, where the names of the noun phrases ran horizontally from left to right (from *first person inclusive duals* to *proper names*) and the grammatical features were displayed vertically from *ego* to *proper*. There was a break between first/second-person pronouns and third-person pronouns, which according to Benveniste were nonindexical persons.

	A	B	C	D	E	F	G	H	I	J	K	L	M	N	O
	1 du incl	1 pl incl	1 singular	1 du excl	1 pl excl	2 singular	2 dual	2 plural	3 du anaphor	3 pl anaphor	3 sg anaphor	3 du demonst	3 pl demonst	3 sg demonst	proper name
a. ego	+	+	+	+	+	-	-	-	-	-	-	-	-	-	-
b. tu	+	+	-	-	-	+	+	+	-	-	-	-	-	-	-
c. unique			+	-	-	+	-	-							
d. plural									+	+	-	+	+	-	
e. enumerable	+	-		+	-		+	-	+	-		+	-		
f. coreferential									+	+	+	-	-	-	-
g. deictic												+	+	+	-
h. proper															+

Figure 1. (Silverstein 2023, 126 reduced)

The most *metapragmatically* transparent noun phrases were those whose rule of use iconically described the indexical use of a token of the noun phrase type that created what it referred to. For example, noun phrases on the left of the hierarchy picked out first-person pronouns referring to the utterer of the token *we*. *We* was a token or replica of a type (an icon) whose object included the person who uttered *we* (an index); it was an example of a creative referential index that created its referential object in the uttering of the token.

Less *metapragmatically* transparent were demonstratives that presupposed but didn't create what they referred to and noun phrases graded by both their indexical iconicity and their metapragmatic transparency. Proper names were in the middle and required a chain of discourse stretching back to a performative baptism or socially sanctioned naming ritual or ceremony. On the right of the hierarchy were noun phrases that referred to natural kinds such as gold or essences such as justice or beauty, whose references were seen as existing independently of uttering the noun phrase. Silverstein showed how the noun phrase hierarchy determined case relationships, nominative/accusative and ergative/absolutive splits, simple and complex clauses, and coreference.

Metapragmatics: Rhetoric, Poetry, and Ritual

His expansion of metapragmatics to include the speech event was most clear in his unpublished paper in 1981, "Metaforces of Power in Traditional Oratory," which also extended metapragmatics to the rhetorical and poetic uses of ritual language. De Man and Silverstein had been influenced by Jakobson's statement that "poetry and metalanguage, however, are in diametrical opposition to each other: in metalanguage the sequence is used to build an equation, whereas in poetry the equation is used to build a sequence" (Jakobson 1960, 358). De Man's metafigural and Silverstein's metapragmatics came up with the same principle that ordered the continuum of rhetorical tropes; both the rhetorization of grammar and metaphorical pseudo-definition involved sequences building equivalences, and the grammatization of rhetoric and metaphorical pseudo-performativity involved equivalences building sequences in the unfolding of discourse.

After identifying the overlap between semantics and metasemantics with glossing (giving definitions), he turned to rhetorical and poetic forms in ritual discourse, which were parts of larger macrocultural and social processes. In his book *Language in Culture*, he juxtaposed "full-tilt ritual" (the Eucharist) to "interaction ritual" (a "getting to know you" ritual between two graduate students at the University of Chicago), pointing out the metrical cadences and rhetorical tropes used in both interactions.

By incorporating the goal-directed use of language into functions of language, he expanded Jakobson's discussions of communicative functions in "Linguistics and Poetics" but also made a connection to social context. Since *pragmatic function*$_1$ included the goal-directed use of speech acts, it included Austin's analysis of performatives, which he extended to ritual discourse. Ritual discourse contained all kinds of rhetorical and poetic uses of language, and in "Metaforces of Power in Traditional Oratory" (Silverstein 1981b) he drew a continuum of rhetorical forms that range from *metaphorical pseudo-definition* (the wise words of the

Western Apache) to *metaphorical pseudo-performativity* (a marriage ritual among the Merina). This continuum extended performativity from Austin's speech acts to ritual discourse and social action: "rituals are actional texts-in-context to read as (conventional) indexical icons. Within a particular cultural universe, rituals 'dynamically figurate' what they effectuate in the space-time context of their performance" (Silverstein in Robbins 2001, 606).

In the "wise words" of the Apache, the referential contents of a definition were played with so *girls are butterflies* was a judgment and not a definitional equivalence among syntagms; it used the same sentence structure as glossing, but since everyone knew that *girls* didn't refer to the same things as *butterflies*, this "pseudo-definition" made a negative judgment: "I don't think butterflies are pretty, but you do, and that made us laugh. It's because they chase around after each other, like they had no work to do, that makes them the same. And that's no good" (Silverstein 1981b, 4-5).

Among the Merina, the *kabary* was a marriage ritual that included the negotiation of a bride price. The groom's side initiated this, and the price was then approved or criticized by the bride's side. If the bride givers criticized it, then the groom's side justified its offer and the reciprocal dialogue continued until the bride's side relented. During the process of the ritual, the bride givers at first used an exclusive *we* and turned to a more inclusive *we* that indicated a growing unity and harmony and settling on the bride price.

However, outside the marriage ritual, the bride's side (wife givers) were inferior in status to wife takers (the groom's side). The unfolding of the ritual was a "reverse diagram" of the social relations between wife givers and takers that was reversed when the marriage ceremony was completed; the kabary was an example of what Silverstein called *metaphorical pseudo-performativity*, whose metapragmatic creativity contrasted to the metasemantic creativity of pseudo-definitions among the "wise words" of the Western Apache. In rituals, the "force of words" was amplified, and there was a performative invocation to macrocosmic forces to change something in the microcosmic ritual situation; all of these played with the interaction between the tropes of metaphor and metonymy and the axes of selection and combination.

The interaction between the tropes of metaphor/metonymy and the axes of selection/combination created a continuum of rhetorical tropes ranging from the metalanguage to the poetic uses of language. The historical background for the discovery of this continuum stretched back to Frege and Tarski, who were mathematical logicians; they had initiated the formal approaches to language by focusing on the semantic and referential functions. The philosopher Rudolph Carnap, the author of *The Logical Syntax of Language* (1934), moved to Prague in 1931 and spoke at the Prague School of Linguistics, where he introduced Jakobson to the problems of metalanguage, including Tarski's writing about truth. Jakobson, always interested in poetry, extended Saussure's definition of the linguistic sign to include the rhetorical and poetic functions of communication. Silverstein revised Jakobson's communicative functions to a more technical definition of metapragmatics, including the $pragmatic_1$ and $pragmatic_2$/$semantic_2$ functions; the $pragmatic_1$ function was the goal-directed use of speech acts, and $pragmatic_2$/$semantic_2$ functions were concerned with indexicality and nonindexicality. De Man, influenced by Jakobson, also extended Tarski to include the rhetorical and poetic functions of language, using Tarski to discover that the "truth" of rhetoric was undecidable. However, Silverstein employed similar arguments for creating a continuum of rhetorical tropes but used them to extend Austin's performativity to ritual discourse and social action. Silverstein then turned to Whorf's research on "fashions of speaking" about time and added that this continuum was anchored by grammatical analogy, which introduced rhetorical ambiguity into grammar. Grammatical analogy was the key idea of Whorf, but the literary side of the linguistic turn didn't pay much attention to this figure who united grammar with the rhetorical and poetic uses of language, overcoming the traditional separation in the trivium among rhetoric, grammar, and logic.

6
Whorf and the Fashion of Speaking About Time

Michael Silverstein and his colleague and student, John Lucy, almost single-handedly revived the Sapir-Whorf hypothesis in linguistic anthropology. Silverstein provided a contemporary linguistic framework and Lucy the experimental evidence for this concept of grammatical mediation of thought and behavior. Silverstein's "Whorfianism and the Linguistic Imagination of Nationality" (2000) and his book *Language in Culture: Lectures on the Social Semiotics of Language* (2023) described the theoretical framework for an update of the Whorfian hypothesis, and the two volumes of John Lucy, *Language Diversity and Thought: A Reformulation of the Linguistic Relativity Hypothesis* (1992) and *Grammatical Categories and Cognition: A Case Study of the Linguistic*

Relativity Hypothesis (1992), provided the empirical evidence supporting it.

The Sapir-Whorf hypothesis was relatively easy to state but much harder to provide experimental proof for. Since our grammatical categories are used every time we speak and are thus our most unconscious and automatic categories, how do they affect our thought and behavior? Sapir and Whorf, influenced by Albert Einstein, expanded the mediation of language to "a new principle of relativity which holds that all observers are not led by the same physical evidence to the same picture of the universe, unless their linguistic backgrounds are similar, or can some way be calibrated" (Whorf 1956, 214).

This relativism has recently been under attack by philosophers such as Max Black and Donald Davidson, linguists such as Chomsky and Ekkehart Malotki, and psychologists such as Steven Pinker. Silverstein showed that most philosophical and psychological critiques of Sapir and Whorf lacked an understanding of comparative linguistics, in which both were trained. Lucy showed that most empirical experiments lacked sufficient methodological control so didn't actually test the Sapir-Whorf hypothesis; he conducted carefully controlled comparative ethnographic experiments in English and Yucatec Mayan that confirmed the grammatical mediation of choice behavior, which supported the hypothesis.

Grammatical Analogy

Most of the philosophical debate was about how relativism was incompatible with contemporary theories of interpretation and understanding while most of the psychological discussion about relativism concerned how to test it. Here I take another route, the relation between grammar and rhetoric. In his famous book *Language*, Sapir identified that grammar was based upon analogy:

> The fact of grammar, a universal trait of language, is simply a generalized expression of the feeling that analogous concepts and relations are most conveniently symbolized in analogous forms. Were a language ever completely "grammatical," it would be a perfect engine of conceptual expression. Unfortunately, or luckily, no language is tyrannically consistent. All grammars leak. (Sapir 1921, 39)

In the classical trivium, logic and grammar were transparent to each other. Grammar produced the sentences that logic evaluated as true or false; an ideal language would be "a perfect engine of conceptual expression," with no ambiguity. However, Sapir's tone was ambivalent about a perfect conceptual language, perhaps because he also wrote poetry.

Analogy is a similarity between two linguistic expressions. It is also a form of indirection, or what Kenneth Burke called "deflection," and the heart of the rhetorical and poetic uses of language. There were two approaches to language in the linguistic turn, and both only focused on the referential function. The literary studies perspective originally came from Saussure's structuralism, which Levi-Strauss extended to myth. Saussure insisted that *langue* (semantic grammar) was separate from *parole* (indexicality) and that the sentence was in *parole* (pragmatics). The other perspective came from transformational linguistics and the analytic philosophy of language, which came from Frege's discovery of quantificational logic and his "sense-reference" distinction. Frege insisted that sentences were either true or false and subject to logical analysis. Since traditionally rhetoric was the use of language for persuasion, it did not belong to langue (Saussure) or logic (Frege) and was not the focus of analysis.

Whorf's argument about the SAE (Standard Average European) "fashion of speaking" was that it has two contradictory notions of time. Mathematical time was the Absolute time of Newton denominated in calendar time and used in science and mathematics; according to Whorf, it came from the count-mass system of European languages. Mathematical time was the framework for all events and was infinitely divisible. However, another notion of time was duration, or the passage of time from future to present to past. Both Newton and Einstein saw that the flow of time was opposed to the mathematical notion of time, which was reversible. Duration was the function of events, and Whorf said it came from verbal tense, which shifted with every moment of speaking; the future and past were calibrated to the present speech event. The bridge between mathematical time and duration was the temporal measure units such as minutes, hours, and days, which connected mathematical time with harmonic oscillation, was measured by pendulums, and was instantiated in mechanical clocks.

Mathematical time was logically *extensional*. An hour measured the same amount of time in sixty minutes, and *sixty minutes* could be substituted for an *hour* in any mathematical or scientific formula without change of truth value for the equation. Mathematical time had constant hours, now based on the vibrations of a cesium atom. For example, sundials had variable nonconstant hours because they varied with the length of daylight and were not extensional. Intensional contexts were where references shifted. Indexicals like *this*, *that*, and verbal tenses changed their references with every new act of speaking; verbs of thinking, feeling, and speaking (*he believes that..., he is angry that..., he promises that...*) and modality also introduced reference shift and were *intensional* contexts. The Western "fashion of speaking" of time combined extensional and intensional notions such that mathematical/extensional time seemed embodied in the flow of indexical/intensional time as duration; the temporal measure units acted as a bridge between mathematical time and duration such that extensional calendar time was instantiated in the flow of time.

Whorf talked about how SAE languages "objectify" nonspatialized and nonperceptible "qualities and potentials": "Our metaphorical system, by naming nonspatial experiences after spatial ones, imputes to sounds, smells, tastes, emotions, and thoughts qualities like the colors, luminosities, shapes, angles, textures, and motions of spatial experience" (Whorf 1956, 155–156). Echoing Sapir on the analogical basis of language, Whorf then introduced art:

> Now European art is distinctive in the way it seeks deliberately to play with synesthesia. Music tries to suggest scenes, color, movement, geometric design; painting and sculpture are often consciously guided by the analogies of music's rhythm; colors are conjoined with feeling for the analogy to concords and discords. The European theater and opera seek a synthesis of many

> arts. It may be that in this way our metaphorical language that was in some sense a confusion of thought is producing, through art, a result of far-reaching value—a deeper esthetic sense leading toward a more direct apprehension of underlying unity behind the phenomena so variously reported by our sense channels. (Whorf 1956, 156)

However, both Newton and Einstein said that *extensional mathematical* time was opposed to our psychological experience of the flow of time, which was *indexical* and logically *intensional.* Whorf saw these contradictory notions combining in the SAE fashion of speaking about time, in which mathematical time was instantiated in the flow of time by temporal measure units like *seconds*, *minutes*, and *hours.* Whorf thought most people in SAE cultures saw Newtonian space, time, and matter as intuitive (as Kant did) and then superseded by the mathematics of relativity. Whorf believed these came from language and culture, not intuition: "The right answer is: Newtonian space, time, and matter are no intuitions. They are recepts from culture and language. That is where Newton got them" (Whorf 1956, 153). Whorf then described how our fashion of speaking about time favored "historicity" and "record keeping," including the mathematics of finance ("records, bookkeeping, accounting") and academic history ("annals, histories, the historical attitude"). But he didn't draw out the implications of these contradictory notions of time.

But what did Whorf mean by grammatical analogy? Whorf was an insurance agent, and he noticed that people are misled by linguistic analogies that lead to accidents or even disasters. For example, if they saw a sign saying "empty gasoline drums," they might act more carelessly around them even though they contained explosive vapor, which was inflammable and even more dangerous than empty drums. He extended these lexical analogies to grammatical analogies and discovered that our form/substance distinction came from the count-mass system for nouns in European languages; for example, Mandarin Chinese did not distinguish between count and mass nouns or have a strong philosophical distinction between form and substance.

A noun clause with a head noun and modifiers (an attributive clause) was like a tree structure for classification. The head noun was at the top of the tree and the grammatical modifiers represented subclassifications. A deeper tree represented a deeper subclassification of the head noun; if grammatical classifications had similar tree structures that classified overlapping things, the grammatical analogy went from the deeper classifications to the shorter ones because the deeper ones represented future possible classifications. For example, the count-mass distinction among European languages distinguished between count nouns that are pluralized directly by cardinal numbers (*three sticks*, *three trees*) and mass nouns that couldn't be pluralized: *three waters** or *three flours** (*=ungrammatical).

Instead, mass nouns required a measure word, as in *three glasses of water*, which made a distinction between the measure units that were substanceless forms and the head noun, joined to the units by *of* and itself a formless substance. Some of the mass nouns with measure units had a clear-cut perceptible difference between form and substance, like *three glasses of water. Three hours* cannot be perceived together; the analogy was from perceptible difference to nonperceptible difference, from *three glasses of water* to *three hours of time*, where an *hour* was a substanceless form (as a measure unit and *time* was a formless substance). Our philosophical form/substance distinction came from this grammatical analogy, which generalized to the SAE form/substance distinction (substanceless forms and formless substances). Time was a formless substance, like space, ready to be countable and infinitely divisible as in Newton's conception of Absolute time and space.

Bringing Together De Man and Silverstein

When De Man came to the University of Chicago in 1979, he didn't meet with Silverstein even though both had been influenced by the linguistic research of Jakobson and Benveniste; perhaps if they had met, the linguistic turn would not have come to the end that Lucy and McEnany described in *Representations*. At that time, Tarski's work had become a strong influence on the analytic philosophy of language through Davidson, who arrived at Chicago in 1976. He championed Tarski's approach to truth and applied it to the problems of meaning and communication. At the end of his life, he wrote "A Nice Derangement of Epitaphs," which argued that prior knowledge of grammar and the logical structure of language faced tremendous difficulties explaining passing moments of mutual interpretations, especially malapropisms and slips of the tongue. These were, of course, examples of rhetorical indirection from normative referential discourse.

Davidson's article was considered a "deconstruction" of his earlier work on semantic approaches to meaning. But it pointed to the problem that was inherent in the separation of rhetoric from grammar and the close philosophical alignment with grammar and logic. Berlant joined with Derrida and De Man, agreeing that focusing on "indirection" was also a call to rethink the trivium and the role of language in society. Tarski's definition of truth only considered the referential function of logic because it was concerned with mathematical truth. However, the meaning of sentences changed as they unfolded in real time; the axis of combination was tied to parole and indexicality and introduced the problems of reference shift and intensionality. De Man's "rhetorization of grammar" and the "grammatization of rhetoric" were *metafigural*; similarly, Silverstein's continuum from "metaphorical pseudo-definition" (metaphor) to "metaphorical pseudo-performativity" (metonymy) was *metapragmatic*.

The "rhetorization of grammar" and "metaphorical pseudo-definition" saw a referential object that has two different interpretations (rhetorical or literal versus two semantic definitions given by glossing), emphasizing the axis of selection holding the axis of combination constant. The "grammatization of rhetoric" and "metaphorical pseudo-performativity" looked at the meaning of equivalences as they interacted across the discourse, as the axis of combination unfolded. Both De Man and Silverstein realized, like Tarski did for mathematical truth, that the pragmatics of the referential function continues in a never-ending hierarchy of metalevels. De Man didn't see that rhetoric or indirection or deflection would be built into grammar, which Silverstein and Lucy understood when they expanded Sapir and Whorf to include grammatical analogy.

7
Between Time and Subjectivity

Grammatical analogy was at the heart of the Sapir-Whorf hypothesis of linguistic relativism. Although Whorf and Silverstein applied the hypothesis of grammatical mediation to the Western notions of time, perhaps the most salient example for Silverstein was performativity, especially the philosopher John Austin's analysis of speech acts. It turned out that performativity was the entry into a whole "folk ideology" of subjectivity, which had ontological implications through its relationships with indexicality and modality and moral implications because promises were the origins of social contract theory. Performativity invoked metalanguage because it referred to what it created, but as Austin pointed out, it also involved ritual as a conventionalized social action. What Silverstein did was extend performativity to ritual and set up a continuum of rhetorical and narrative forms along a range that stretched from indexical time (direct speech) to mathematical time (the view from nowhere exemplified in mathematical or scientific writing).

Frege tapped into this folk ideology when he chose indirect discourse for his inquiries into sense and reference, which only focused on the semantic and referential functions. This section will extend his analysis to reach a full description of our fashions of speaking about subjectivity and time that is given in the "horizontal" and "vertical" dimensions of figure 2. The horizontal dimension started with indirect discourse and moved across verbs of speaking, feeling, and thinking. They all had nominal complements with consistent tense/aspect grammatical relationships, so it seemed that everything one could think, one could say—a version of the Western mind-body dualism; the nominal complements were introduced by a subordinating conjunction *that* so that verbs of speaking, feeling, and thinking seemed to be conveying a proposition.

1. speaking verb: *She said that she would go right now.*
2. feeling verb: *She hoped that she would go right now.*
3. mental act: *She decided that she would go right now.*
4. mental state: *She thought that she would go right now.*

However, other rhetorical and narrative forms besides indirect discourse (like direct speech, quotation, and free indirect style) contained a continuum of rhetorical forms that range from indexical speech to the mathematical time of third-person omniscient narration.

1. direct speech: *I will go right now.*
2. quotation: *She said, "I will go right now."*
3. free indirect style: *She said she would go right now.*
4. indirect discourse: *She said that she would go immediately then.*

Free indirect style, which Berlant used for the formulation of cruel optimism, translated the indexical expressivity of the former into a third-person indirect discourse: *She said ugh, she would go right now → She said that she had reluctantly gone immediately.* In figure 2, what were called *de dicto* readings of indirect discourse were from the view of the speaker. *De re* readings were from an objective standpoint. The sentence *Oedipus wanted to marry his mother* could be true because *Jocasta* and *Oedipus's mother* referred to the same person regardless of Oedipus's subjective state. The de dicto readings, which were associated with subjectivity, assumed the falsity of the substitution of *Oedipus's mother* for *Jocasta* in the sentence *Oedipus wanted to marry Jocasta.* The de re was a form of indirect discourse from an objective perspective and true; it assumed an omniscient reporter didn't care that the speaker didn't know that *Oedipus's wife* and *Jocasta* were coreferential. If de re readings were objective, then the "vertical dimension" moved from the indexical time of direct speech to mixed forms in free indirect discourse, to the extensional time of de re modality (figure 2). The similarity of the de re and de dicto readings of indirect discourse were responsible for Frege's distinction of sense and reference in epistemic contexts.[3]

Grammatical Analogy: The Vertical Dimension

There was a metasemantic "vertical" dimension in the nominal complements of verbs of thinking, feeling, and speaking that ranged from direct speech to omniscient narration and moved from the indexical time of direct speech to the extensional time of de re modality and the view from nowhere. For example, one could embed nominal complements for infinite length: *Tom believes that Sally knows that Jerry said that...* This vertical dimension was created by the recursion of nominal complements, each metalevel referring to an object level; reporting speech ranged from the indexicality of free speech and direct quotation to the different styles of third-person narration and reached omniscient narration and the "voice from nowhere."

It extended to the recursion of metalevels that Tarski identified in the liar's paradox.

The voice from nowhere in Western narration was in "homogenous, empty time"; it was presupposed by de re readings of identity statements because they were objective and not from any speakers' perspectives; they ranged from third-person narration to mathematical or logical proofs. There were regular rules of conversion from free speech and direct quotation to indirect discourse, creating a vertical dimension that ranged from the indexicality of direct speech and direct quotation to the temporal modulations of free indirect style and indirect discourse and to abstract time in de re modality. The pivot was the report of speech, which united the vertical and horizontal dimensions.

The indexical basis for subjectivity was shown in direct and indirect discourse and free indirect style, whereas the transition between possibility and necessity turned out to be an interplay between causality and communication. Intensional contexts for subjectivity were counterfactual alternatives for people; but how much could a person change before he became unrecognizable? The intensionality of intentionality was limited to the actual world, whereas in the Fregean examples Galileo didn't know that the morning star and evening star named the same star or Oedipus didn't know that Jocasta was his mother.

An example of the interaction between the horizontal and vertical dimensions of metapragmatics was the discourse of modality. After the work of philosophers like Ruth Barcan Marcus, Saul Kripke, and David Lewis, modal logic was concerned with not just counterfactual alternatives in the actual world but possible worlds in which people could have been different "people"; beyond the initial baptism, they lived different lives. Possible worlds were *counterfactual worlds* in which people could have different narrative histories than in the actual world; the problem was how we attached these alternative subjectivities to the same people. How did we distinguish a possible world in which *Shakespeare* could have died at birth but couldn't have been a hot dog? How did we delimit counterfactual worlds so that not everything goes? Was the "metamodernist" multiverse of *Spider Man: No Way Home* or *Everything, Everywhere All at Once* intelligible?[4] This led to a modal revolution, which made clear some of the metapragmatic principles of Silverstein's noun phrase hierarchy, especially the role of proper names.

How did we advance our talk about modality from counterfactual alternatives in the actual world to the logical structure of possible worlds? Kripke's answer was a *rigid designator*, a proper name that picked out the same person in every possible world; they could live alternative lives in these possible worlds compared to the actual world. Rigid designation relied upon an initial baptism or christening followed by a causal chain of coreference. In our world, *William Shakespeare* rigidly designated him; *Shakespeare* referred to the infant that was christened William Shakespeare by his parents, John Shakespeare and Mary Arden, and there existed a causal chain of coreference to that baptism. *William Shakespeare* could have been a farmer rather than a playwright or could have died in infancy from smallpox, but he couldn't have been a hot dog. *Shakespeare* could have different biographies, and each subjectivity attributed to him (via direct or indirect discourse) could be different because of different indexical histories. But each third-person attribution of subjectivity in indirect discourse (*Shakespeare believed that...*) would be an intensional statement that was a report of what he might have indexically said or thought.

The logical analysis of de re modality allowed philosophers to do a formal analysis of possible worlds; a discussion of counterfactual alternatives in the actual world became a logical analysis, including Kripke's performative analysis of proper names. The shift from counterfactual alternatives in the actual world to possible worlds was a minor linguistic change that had significant philosophical impact and caught a cultural wave of metamodernism in literature and cinema. If *Shakespeare* could have been a farmer, he would have had a completely different subjectivity and a different biographical history from the playwright. Yet these were all different personalities that could have evolved from the infant christened *William Shakespeare*. Causality and communication (the initial baptism and chains of coreference) interacted to rigidly identify an infant as *William Shakespeare* so that the counterfactual alternatives happened to him rather than someone else.

The roots of the relationship between causality and communication were in Peirce's theory of the sign. Causality was a "secondness," the realm of reaction and resistance; signs were "thirdnesses," but every actual sign had an "embodiment" that was determined by causality. If a sign was an interpretant that occurred in a "mind," then it had a "subjective" element dependent upon the interaction between causality and semiosis. This reappeared in modality, where rigid designation was the interaction between causal chains of coreference and an initial performative baptism.

The transition between necessity and possible worlds (all encoded in nominal complements such as *it is necessary that or it is possible that*) required distinguishing between causal and communicative relationships. Kripke argued that necessary identities presupposed logical or causal relationships. Proper names combined them: a performative baptism and a causal chain of coreference that stretched back to the original naming ceremony. For a natural kind like *water*, if *water* = H_2O was true in all possible worlds, then it was a necessary truth; water and H_2O didn't shift reference and were intersubstitutable salva veritate. The omniscient narrator and the voice from nowhere operated in de re modality; this is captured in the vertical dimension of figure 2, where it ranged from the indexical time of direct speech to de re modality with the voice from nowhere in extensional time.

Grammatical Analogy: The Horizontal Dimension

The horizontal dimension included the nominal complements shared among verbs of thinking, speaking, and feeling and created relationships among indexicality, subjectivity, and modality. For every metalevel that the nominal complements created on the vertical dimension, there were similar "decalages" among the verbs of thinking, feeling, and speaking given by their shared tense and aspect relations. Verbs of speaking (performative verbs), mental act and state verbs, and verbs of feeling all shared a reluctance to use the present progressive and took nominal (propositional) complements introduced in English by *that* and *to*. The sharing of tense and aspect meant almost a complete transference among what was thought, spoke, and felt; these tense/aspect grammatical analogies interacted with the nominal complements, which represented different levels of abstraction: indexicality, subjectivity, and modality. These two grammatical analogies created a "linguistic holding environment of subjectivity" that Jakobson and Silverstein saw as extending from the rigors of logic and mathematics to the creativity of poetry.

Austin incorporated sense and reference into his definition of the locutionary act, and illocutionary force came from Frege's notion of *kraft* (force, energy, power). The ways of reporting speech were closely tied to illocutionary verbs; indirect discourse was introduced by illocutionary (metapragmatic) verbs and the Fregean-style sentences about the morning and evening stars could be rewritten as *Galileo said that the morning star was the evening star* and would still be intensional. Austin originally identified performatives by grammatical criteria and noticed that performative verbs had a reluctance to use the present progressive to express an ongoing act: *I hereby promise to...* vs. *I am hereby promising to...*, *I hereby name this baby...* vs. *I am hereby naming this baby....* Besides tense and aspect being the basis for grammatical analogies across verbs of thinking, speaking, and feeling, these verbs shared an additional feature: they take nominal complements introduced by subordinating conjunctions (such as *that* in English, *dass* in German, *che* in Italian, or *que* in French or Spanish) or infinitive constructions such as *I hereby promise to....* These nominal complements were intensional contexts that ranged in abstraction from indexicality to necessity.

Expanding on Austin's linguistic prerequisites for performativity, Silverstein summarized the grammatical criteria for performatives: a speaker uttered to an addressee a metapragmatic verb that was unmarked for tense (the present), aspect (perfective, nonprogressive), and modality (declarative), had a complement clause introduced by *that* or *to*, and created what it referred to. Austin and Silverstein didn't point out that mental state verbs (including epistemic and affective mental states like *know* and *believe* or *fear* and *hope*) and mental act verbs (*decide*, *recognize*) had the same reluctance to use the progressive aspect to report an ongoing act: *I believe that...* vs. *I am believing that...*, *I know that...* vs. *I am knowing that...*; verbs of feeling such as hope or fear: *I fear that...* vs. *I am fearing that...*; mental acts: *I decide that...* vs. *I am deciding that....* These grammatical analogies created the sense that speaking, thinking, and feeling were intertranslatable.

In his reformulation of performatives, Austin came up with a six-way classification of illocutionary acts that took similar propositional complements:

1. verdictives (*rank, grade*)
2. exercitives (*order, request*)
3. commissives (*promise, undertake*)
4. behabitives (*congratulate, commend*)
5. operatives (*appoint, nominate*)
6. expositives (*state, declare*)

The philosopher Zeno Vendler noticed that this typology had grammatical counterpart categories in mental act and state verbs; almost everything that could be thought could be said and vice versa. For example, corresponding to a performative "commissive" such as *promise*, there was the mental act "resolutive" *decide* and the mental state "conative" *want*. We could reconstruct a performative utterance as starting with mental states like *believe* or *desire*, a mental act of *deciding* between alternatives, and then issuing a performative act of *promising*. A mental process started with the contemplation of mental states, formed an intention as a mental act, and then issued a performative utterance. It was a simulacrum of the mind-body dualism, and this "folk theory" of subjectivity was created by grammatical classifications and analogies among thinking, speaking, and feeling, which interacted with the tenses and aspects of narration (direct and indirect discourse). The translation across verbs of thinking (both mental states and mental acts), feeling, and speaking in the horizontal dimension was given by their tense-aspect relations, leading to the easy transposition in European languages from inner thought to direct speech. Everything that can be thought also can be spoken, and the nominal complements encode the fashion of speaking about time.

Besides having cross-cutting grammatical analogies that produced the mind-body dualism, verbs of thinking, speaking, and feeling also had nominal complement clauses that encoded modality, subjectivity, and indexicality. These nominal complements reinforced the mind-body dualism, a body that worked in the physical world and a mind that operated and communicated with mental entities (propositions) ranging in abstraction from causality to the mental:

> Man lives in two environments, in two worlds: as a "body," and "extended thing," he is among objects and events in the physical, spatio-temporal universe: as a "mind," a "thinking thing," he lives and communes with objects of a different kin, which he also perceives, acquires, holds, and offers in various ways to other citizens, to other minds. (Vendler 1972, 34)

Intensional contexts also interacted with the grammatical analogies between mental and feeling states, mental acts, and performatives (actions). Mental and feeling states like *believe*, *know*, and *hope* were states and had no event properties. A mental act verb like *decide* combined a belief and desire into an intention, and intention distinguished action from behavior and led to a choice and an action like the issuance of a performative. Mental state → mental act → intention → performative action (*I believe that... I decide that... I intend that... I promise that...*) reproduced the mind-body dualism. We inhabited a world of thoughts and propositions that we communicated to other people and also a world of material things and objects; since we could think of things in the same ways we could talk about them, we saw modality, subjectivity, and indexicality as three principal philosophical dimensions that applied to things and people.

Metapragmatics mediated the logical regimentation of language with its desire for referential accuracy and the rhetorical and poetic uses of language that played with indirection. The logical regimentation of language had been the focus of the analytic philosophers; the same forms of indirect discourse were also the focus of narrative and poetic experiments by writers and poets. Austin's discovery of performativity was the "transparent" window into how language faced both directions, as indicated by the interest in performativity in both the philosophy of language and literary studies. It's not surprising that Austin started with performatives and that the legacy of the linguistic turn continued not in issues like "différance" or the "arche-sign" but in the performativity of gender and identity.

Summarizing the interaction between the vertical and horizontal dimensions of our "fashions of speaking" about subjectivity and time, first there was a general pattern of syntactically encoded similarities between verbs of speaking and verbs of thinking such that they seemed to be almost interchangeable expressions. Second, there was a decrease in the degree to which expressive presentations of subjectivity were allowed across all the verbs of speaking and thinking as one moved from direct quotation to sentences containing parentheticals (Ugh, *she thought*) to indirect discourse. Third, as one moved from direct quotation and sentence parentheticals to indirect discourse, there was also an increase in the "objectivity" of the complement clause by dropping the expressive and indexical elements.

The de dicto interpretations of direct and indirect quotations and subject-oriented parentheticals were attributable to the "source" of the quote or original thought; speaker-oriented parentheticals also had only a de dicto reading. However, the de re reading of indirect discourse was independent of the source's consciousness and seemed to present an objective proposition in the complement clause that can be grasped by de dicto subjective interpretations of different speakers and thinkers. The behavior of these forms of reporting speech and thought also interacted with modal differences that introduced similar de dicto and de re distinctions, leading to a graded set of forms ranging from the objectivity of necessary truths to the subjectivity of "inner" thoughts.

Our fashion of speaking of time was the intersection of an extensional notion of absolute time and indexical tense: an infinitely divisible and extensional time and an indexical and intensional *duration* that flowed smoothly among past, present, and future. The abstract notion of absolute time, which we learn in science in school, represented time as an infinitely divisible time line in which all events took place. The concept of time was represented in the head noun of temporal measure phrases, *three hours of time*; it has changed over history, moving from theological time with inconstant indexical hours to absolute extensional time with constant hours. But all of them represented what was referred to as the head noun *time* as a "spatial formless continuum" derived from our count-mass system of SAE languages.

However, the measure units such as *seconds*, *minutes*, *hours*, and *days* bridged our everyday talk about indexical and mathematical times; they calibrated our abstract notions of time with natural physical movements so that "homogenous, empty time" was instantiated in the flow of time. One historical transition was the development of constant hours, which were necessary for an extensional notion of abstract time. The development of constant hours mapped the "flow of time" given by the tense system upon regular natural displacements, such as the pendulum or spring mechanisms of mechanical clocks.

The Continuum of Rhetorical and Narrative Genres

The following figure 2 combines the vertical (metasemantic) and horizontal (metapragmatic) dimensions. The vertical dimension from free speech to de re modality ranged from indexical expressivity of quotation to third-person omniscient narration and from indexical intensional time to mathematical extensional time. The boldfaced horizontal dimension ranged across the nominal complements and tense/aspect relationships that united verbs of thinking, feeling, and speaking (mental states → feeling verbs → mental acts → performatives) so that everything thought and felt had counterparts in mental act verbs and speech acts; it explained the easy transposition in European languages from inner thought and speech to speech acts, as if external speech was the communication of inner thoughts.

1. Free speech:
   Oedipus: I'm marrying Jocasta tomorrow. **(direct speech)**
2. Direct quotation:
   Oedipus said, "I'm marrying Jocasta tomorrow." **(verb of speaking)**
   Oedipus decided, "I'm marrying Jocasta tomorrow." **(mental act)**
   Oedipus hoped, "I'm marrying Jocasta tomorrow." **(feeling verb)**
   Oedipus thought, "I'm marrying Jocasta tomorrow." **(mental state)**
3. Free indirect style:
   Oedipus said that he would marry Jocasta tomorrow. **(verb of speaking)**
   He would marry Jocasta tomorrow, Oedipus said. **(verb of speaking)**
   Oedipus decided that he would marry Jocasta tomorrow. **(mental act)**
   He would marry Jocasta tomorrow, Oedipus decided. **(mental act)**
   Oedipus hoped that he would marry Jocasta tomorrow. **(feeling verb)**
   Oedipus thought he would marry Jocasta tomorrow. **(mental state)**
4. Indirect discourse:
   Oedipus said that he would marry Jocasta the next day. **(verb of speaking)**
   Oedipus decided that he would marry Jocasta the next day. **(mental act)**
   He would marry Jocasta the next day, Oedipus decided. **(mental act)**
   Oedipus hoped that he would marry Jocasta the next day. **(feeling verb)**
   Oedipus thought he would marry Jocasta the next day. **(mental state)**
5. De dicto reading:
   Oedipus said that he would marry Jocasta. True **(verb of speaking)**
   Oedipus said that he would marry his mother. False **(verb of speaking)**
6. De re reading: verb of speaking, third-person omniscient narration
   Oedipus said that he would marry Jocasta. True **(verb of speaking)**
   Oedipus said that he would marry his mother. True **(verb of speaking)**
7. Modality: the view from nowhere, third-person omniscient narration:
   It was possible that Oedipus would marry Jocasta. True **(modality)**
   It was possible that Oedipus would marry his mother. True **(modality)**
   It was necessary that Oedipus would marry Jocasta. False **(modality)**
   It was necessary that Oedipus would marry his mother. False **(modality)**

   Apostrophe would fit between direct quotation and free indirect style.

Figure 2.

The fashion of speaking about time interacted with our fashion of speaking about subjectivity. The extensional notion of time interacted with the grammatical structuring of verbs of thinking, feeling, and speaking to produce the belief-desire model of decision making under uncertainty, which was the dominant model of subjectivity in the social sciences and analytic philosophy; perhaps it was best articulated in the work of the philosopher Donald Davidson. The indexical notion of time interacted with that same fashion of speaking encoded in our verbs of thinking, feeling, and speaking to produce "flow models" of subjectivity, perhaps best represented by Mikhail Csikszentmihalyi and Henri Bergson. The flow model started with time as a function of events; in this case, it was the speech event, which anchored the flow of tenses from the future, through the present, and into the past.

8
The Linguistic Turn of *Cruel Optimism*

This section will introduce Berlant's effort to create a Marxist approach to a semiotics of affect and subjectivity. Previous sections explored Postone's treadmill structure of relative surplus value to understand its relationship to cruel optimism. It connected the fetish to a continuum of narrative styles and rhetorical forms that formed the link between value and language. The continuum of narrative and rhetorical forms translated value into the fetish, and the fetish translated into narrative and rhetorical forms that created the treadmill structure of cruel optimism. Using Henri Bergson's accounts of time and duration, the conclusion outlines Berlant's creation of a "flow model" of subjectivity as an alternative to decision making under uncertainty.

Berlant started with what Postone omitted and Silverstein only touched upon in his analysis of the linguistic roots of national subjectivity: affect. In her introduction to *Cruel Optimism*, Berlant said that she would analyze the "contemporary moment from within that moment," echoing Marx's opening of *Capital* where the capitalism of his day appeared "as an 'immense collection of commodities.'" But instead of starting with the commodity, Berlant said that the present was first perceived affectively. Then what was her relationship to Marx's analysis of *Capital*?

Although she was a colleague of Postone's for thirty years, she only made passing reference to him in her books. But perhaps a clue was given in her colleague and coauthor Sianne Ngai's book, *Theory of the Gimmick: Aesthetic Judgment and Capitalist Form*, which used Postone's "treadmill" analysis of relative surplus value as one of its major theoretical points. Postone's account of relative surplus value was of an accelerating creative destruction caused by technological innovation. In Marxist terminology, innovation caused the productivity of labor to go up, requiring less time to produce more commodities; the result was a growing contradiction between value and wealth (less abstract labor time to produce a commodity but more commodities per abstract hour) and a falling rate of profit.

Ngai emphasized how the gimmick embodied this contradiction: "overrated devices that strike us as working too little (labor-saving tricks) but also as working too hard (strained efforts to get our attention)" (Ngai 2020, 1); innovation reduced the value of labor but needed public acceptance to spread.

Berlant, however, focused on another aspect of the treadmill effect that Postone described. Cruel optimism and the treadmill effect had a similar temporal structure in which people were attached to long-term capitalist fantasies of the good life in ways that threatened their everyday existence in the present. Postone described the treadmill effect from a theoretical standpoint as a dialectic of abstract and concrete time that produced the historical present. Berlant started from the historical present ("Cruel optimism is... a deictic") and articulated the tension between the fantasies of neoliberal capitalism (the dreams of more wealth or success) and getting through the everyday.

The treadmill as an image works at both levels. Think of a treadmill, an elliptical machine, or a stationary bike as an example of cruel optimism. People bought them and looked forward to keeping fit over the months when they would be cooped up during the COVID-19 lockdowns. Each day, they monitored their heart rate, how much they ran, and the time it took. The measurements went up and down but as long as the spread trended upward, they were satisfied. Perhaps every other week, they increased the pace, pushing themselves in the dreams of keeping fit and perhaps even losing weight. But then they visited the doctor in preparation for a post-COVID recovery and were told that although they had lost a few pounds, their knees were wearing out; dreams of a good life (losing weight or keeping fit) "are an obstacle to flourishing."

Of course, this example was a bit tongue-in-cheek, but the analogy was to our attachment to the treadmill of relative surplus value and contemporary capitalism, i.e., to creative destruction in its contemporary form. As we accelerated the rate of innovation, we undermined the value of our labor input. Relative surplus value, while promising the neoliberal fantasies of the "good life," concomitantly devalued the labor power needed to produce that material wealth. To the extent we were "attached" to the dreams of a "good life" in neoliberalism, we were devaluing our own labor while we chased after dreams of material wealth. This was the meaning of cruel optimism writ large, which looked at the treadmill from a slightly different angle than that of Sianne's gimmick and followed the trajectory of innovations. Innovations increase the productivity of labor but degrade value in the name of wealth; at the same time, people "make strained efforts to get our attention" to buy them, allowing them to spread and lowering the socially necessary labor time needed to reproduce the worker.

But why apostrophe and free indirect style as the tropes for analyzing the treadmill structure of cruel optimism? Why not irony or allegory? Berlant turned to Johnson's work on apostrophe and free indirect style because it explored "a way to think about the strange temporalities of projection into an enabling object that is also disabling" (Berlant 2011, 25)—the affective spread between our expectations of the good life and how they undermine our day-to-day existence. A treadmill also enabled while disabling—each step forward was matched by an opposite displacement but at the same time, the person hadn't moved. Varying the speed would change the magnitude of the displacement per unit of abstract time—a microcosm of the "historical present" where value is denominated in absolute time but labor efficiency is in the here and now of "concrete historical time." The speed created a spread of displacement—a treadmill was not directional but an example of "living in the spread." Varying speeds changed the magnitude of the spreads per unit of absolute time; a treadmill captured the basic idea of volatility as "the propensity to continually change one's current state, irrespective of the direction of the change" (Derman 2023, 1). Perhaps the treadmill was Postone's gimmick—it combined pithiness and generativity while not moving anywhere.

Free Indirect Style, Apostrophe, and the Fetish

Free indirect style was also often considered to be an "odd storytelling trick" in which "the narrator temporarily takes a backseat for the sake of better representing the consciousness of the character, though the reader still relied on that third-person middleman to tell the story" (Gingerich 2012, 1). Linguistically, it contrasted with direct and indirect discourse, standard ways of representing the speech and thoughts of other people. Comparing the following sentences shows several grammatical differences between direct and indirect speech that also hold across German, French, and Spanish and were representative of SAE.

1. Direct: Mary said to me yesterday at the station, "I will meet you here tomorrow."

Indirect: Mary said to me yesterday at the station that she would meet me there today.

One could transform the direct form into the indirect by:

1. removing the quotation marks (or the introductory pause between reporting and reported clauses in speech) and inserting subordinating conjunctions such as *that*, *if*, or *whether* in English

2. shifting the grammatical persons (personal or possessive pronouns, determiners, and verbal person) from first or second in direct speech to the third person in indirect discourse: *I* → *she*
3. applying concordance of tense rules to the verbs of subordinate clauses in indirect discourse; typically, there is a back-shifting of tenses
4. converting spatial and temporal deictic elements: *here* → *there tomorrow* → *today* (Lee 1997, 202-3)

Free indirect style had the third-person pronoun and tense of indirect discourse but the indexical subjectivity of direct discourse.

1. Direct discourse: Mary said, "If only I could leave!"
2. Indirect discourse: Mary said that she wanted/wished to leave.
3. Free indirect discourse: If only she could leave!
4. Free indirect discourse: If only she could leave, she thought.

Yet unlike omniscient third-person narration, which occurred in precapitalist texts such as the Bible, free indirect style was publicly introduced into novelistic discourse by Flaubert at the same time as manufacturing capitalism was developing (*Madame Bovary* was written at the same time as Marx's *Grundrisse*) and was often considered the "hallmark of the modern novel." Direct and indirect discourse kept the boundaries of the third-person narrator and the characters' speech and thoughts separated in different clause structures. Free indirect style juxtaposed two voices in a single utterance with the objectivity of third-person narration and the indexical subjectivities of the characters; this was the narrative equivalent of Postone's historical present, in which the nonindexical third person was the frame but the indexical voices were the content. Perhaps it's not surprising that its overuse could seem gimmicky, as if it was "working too hard."

From a semiotic standpoint the novel was a microcosm of the ways of representing time, as in Bakhtin's notion of "chronotope." Narration consisted of narrating and narrated-about events, all of which occurred in and were measurable by the absolute time of clocks and calendars; absolute time was the framework for all events, including mental events. Externally, novels were commodities and as such were subject to the absolute time of relative surplus value. But internally the novel contained different levels of time, ranging from the indexicality of direct discourse through indirect discourse, and omniscient narration with its "view from nowhere" in abstract calendar time.

Free indirect discourse played with these temporal levels, mixing the objectivity of the third person with the indexicality of the *I-you* axis. The narrator's voice acted as a mediator between the external and internal senses of time; free indirect style could mix the times of the indexical expressivities of the narrated-about's characters and the nonindexical third-person narrator. Free indirect style also played with the hierarchy of times by mixing time and personhood, forcing "the reader to transact a different, more open relation of unfolding to what she is reading, judging, being, and thinking she understands" (Berlant 2011, 26). It made the indexical *I-you* axis interact with the nonindexical third person. If the third person represented the possibility of an omniscient narrator moving in extensional abstract time, free indirect style "punctuated" that third person with the indexical expressiveness of face-to-face communication.

But how did the chronotope of the novel interact with the "chronotope of value"? As the Frankfurt School quickly discovered, fetishism was the mediator between an economic theory of value and its social and cultural implications. Fetishism did not appear in the *Grundrisse* or *A Contribution to the Critique of Political Economy* because it was a fundamental concept in a historically specific immanent critique that was only present in volume I of *Capital*; it was a necessary component of people's attachment to capitalism, in which they saw social relations in "the fantastic form of a relation between things." Marx called it a "Hieroglyphe" that has to be deciphered; from a rhetorical standpoint, the simple form of value, which contained Marx's account of fetishism, was a combination of metaphor (exchange value) and metonymy (use value) that appeared in the fetish as "material relations between persons and social relations between things." The simple form of exchange was between two "equal" commodities, and the equivalence was similar to metaphor or glossing, which involved comparing or equating equivalences.

The forms of value had a vertical dimension of abstract metalevels. Abstract labor time was created from the quantitative equivalences of two commodities. The simple form was the equivalence of two commodities; the total form was the expansion, where the relative form had many forms of commodities for which it could be exchanged; and the general form was the reverse, where many commodities could be exchanged for one equivalent. Money was simply silver or goods replacing the general form as money, the quantitative medium of exchange. The horizontal dimension of exchange met the vertical dimension when money-mediated exchanges were dominant and most commodities were produced for exchange. Surplus value or capital added another metalevel accompanied by the horizontal dimensions of C-M-C and M-C-M' (the expression for surplus value), which represented the money-mediated circulation of value and surplus value.

Value, or abstract labor time, was the creation of a third-person or abstract quantitative mediation between exchanges; in a communication model, its equivalent was the creation of third-person narration, which involved a third-person narrator who was not present in the original exchange of communication. The dialectic of abstract mathematical time and indexical time was captured in figure 2 from the move from indexical expressivity of direct speech to the subjectivity of indirect discourse to modality in the mathematical time of third-person omniscient narration. Its linguistic form was indirect discourse, which in third-person narration transformed the indexical expressivity of the *I-you* axis to third-person reported discourse. The fetish was as if everything was looked at through third-person narration, changing the indexical expressivity of the speaker and hearer into the tense and person of third-person indirect discourse. However, free indirect style inverted indirect discourse by keeping the person and tense of third-person narration but then quoted the indexical expressivity of the *I-you* axis. Apostrophe took the absent third person as an addressee (or treated the addressee as a third person) and played with the affects between persons.

The money dialectic started with the simple form of value, which was the exchange of commodities between two agents, i.e., the *I-you* axis of subjective agency. The money form mediated all *I-you* exchanges and represented abstract labor time, which was abstracted from metaphorical equivalences. In capitalism, everything was produced to be exchanged so that simple exchanges were mediated by money and value. There was a similar relationship between the *I-you* axis and third-person narration. Indirect discourse converted the subjectivity of the *I-you* axis into third-person forms. The third person was the nonperson or as Benveniste pointed out, was not indexical; it referred to people who weren't being addressed.

Indirect discourse in third-person omniscient narration translated the fetish into narrative terms by removing any signs of the indexical subjectivity of the people narrated about. Free indirect style subjectified omniscient narration by providing the person and tense of indirect discourse, but with the subjectivity of the *I-you* axis. Apostrophe further subjectified free indirect style by providing a second person to address. The fetishism of money made the *I-you* exchanges seem mediated by money and value, i.e., relationships of things replaced relationships among the agents. The rhetoric of time "translated" the absolute time of abstract labor time into the fetish; the fetish was the form of appearance of the *historical time* of relative surplus value, and then free indirect style and apostrophe translated the fetish into the *historical present* of affects and emotions.

Relative surplus value was the dialectic of abstract and concrete labor times. However, unlike in absolute surplus value, concrete labor time had a crucial role in relative surplus value because it determined the efficiency of labor that drove innovation. Innovations were qualitative social inventions that reduced the abstract time needed to produce commodities but depended upon the qualitative social breakthroughs that previous innovation had created. As Postone said, the efficiency of labor "is grounded in the social character of the use value dimension of labor" that "expresses the notion of (abstract) time" (Postone 1993, 293). The dialectic of abstract and concrete labor times created the treadmill structure of relative surplus, and cruel optimism transformed it into the affective instantiation of creative destruction.

In the fetish, one transformed the expressivity of face-to-face communication into a communication between priced commodities. Free indirect style began to dismantle the linguistic version of the fetish by reintroducing indexical subjectivity but in a new form. It contained both the extensional time of the third person and the expressivity of indexical time–which was the rhetorical analog to the dialectic of abstract and concrete labor time in relative surplus value that was calibrated to abstract calendar time, but with the social hour filled by material wealth generated by concrete labor time. This was where free indirect style overlapped with apostrophe. It was if "the open relation of unfolding" in free indirect style prepared the "objective" third-person narratives for subjective cathexis and then apostrophe provided the attachment.

Apostrophe and Free Indirect Style

In "Apostrophe, Animation, and Abortion," Johnson described apostrophe as a form of "turning aside" that "manipulates the *I/Thou* structure of *direct* address in an indirect, fictionalized way" (Johnson 1986, 30). This was a general effect of apostrophe, as Johnson showed in her analyses of materials as different as Percy Shelley's *Ode to the West Wind* and Gwendolyn Brooks's *Mother*. Drawing upon Benveniste's analysis of pronouns, Johnson discovered in *Mother* ("Abortions will not let you forget") an opening line that addressed *you* but contained no *I* as "representing the self as eternally addressed and possessed by the lost, anthropomorphized other" (Johnson 1986, 32).

The "you" in the opening lines can be seen as an "I" that has become alienated, distanced from itself, and combined with a generalized other, which includes and feminizes the reader of the poem. The grammatical I/thou starting point of traditional apostrophe has been replaced by a structure in which the speaker is simultaneously eclipsed, alienated, and confused with the addressee. It is already clear that something has happened to the possibility of establishing a clear-cut distinction in this poem between subject and object, agent and victim. (Johnson 2014, 222)

Berlant translated these comments into a general interpretation of apostrophe that delineated the interaction between the markedness relationships between grammatical personhood and affect, in a breathtaking synthesis of affect theory and linguistic mediation:

> Apostrophe therefore appears to be a reaching out to a you, a direct movement from place x to place y, but it is actually a turning back, an animating of a receiver on behalf of the desire to make something happen now that realizes something in the speaker, makes the speaker more or differently possible, because she has admitted, in a sense, the importance of speaking for, as, and to, two—but only under the

> condition, and illusion, that the two are really (in) one. (Berlant 2011, 26)

But the *I-you* axis of apostrophe also anchored the present moment of speaking, where the voice addressed the other but was really speaking to itself. It played upon the grammatical features of markedness that Benveniste first discovered, Johnson used, and Berlant expanded upon.

In figure 1, *we* on the *I-you* axis (first-person plurals) was placed horizontally left of *I* (the first-person singular), which was left of the *he*, *she*, or *they*, the third-personal pronouns. There was a markedness gradient from the left and right horizontal dimension that ranged from the metapragmatic transparency of pluralized first-person pronouns to the abstract essences like "beauty" or "justice" that were not indexical. These grammatical features were the backbone of the hierarchy of narrative genres in figure 2: free speech (the *I-you* axis) was at the bottom of the vertical dimension of the hierarchy, with third-person-oriented indirect discourse in the middle; de readings overlapped with third-person omniscient narration, and modality had the "voice from nowhere" and third-person omniscient narration.

Berlant's play with apostrophe and free indirect style revealed that affect interacted with the hierarchy of linguistic features. Apostrophe as a rhetorical device used the grammatical markings of the pronouns so that they appeared in opposition ("speaking for, as, and to, two") as marked pairs of the contrast between speaker and receiver but "only under the condition, and illusion, that two were really (in) one." Apostrophe played with the distinction that *we* was placed left of *I* in the noun phrase hierarchy and "personalized" it as if they "are really (in) one." *I*'s subjectivity presupposed the *we* and prepared the split of markings in free indirect style, which contained the indexical expressivity of the *I-you* axis while maintaining the person and tense of the third person of indirect discourse. Berlant invoked the hierarchy of narrative and rhetorical forms that range from the indexicality of the *I-you* axis of direct speech to the *I* to the third-person narrator; it also traveled from the indexicality of time anchored in verbal tense to mathematical time, which was the formal analog to the time of modality.

Rhetoric, in the form of grammatical analogy, did not have the function of persuasion but "indirectly" directed the "flow" of semantic meanings from one set of referents to another. The hierarchy of narrative styles and rhetorical forms directed the flow of affect across direct speech, apostrophe, free indirect style, and third-person narration. Indirection also became the use of tropes in context, creating the bivalent social affects of both cruel optimism and the gimmick. Following Peirce, Derrida, and De Man, believing that pure rhetoric was not the perlocutionary effect of logic (locution) and grammar (illocution) for persuasion but rather the process by which signs gave birth to other signs or "the flow of signs," rhetoric made the dialectic of time underlying contemporary capitalism true in practice.[5]

9
Berlant's Flow Model of Subjectivity

Berlant didn't use Bergson's arguments criticizing mathematics, language, and cinema for using the "cinematographic illusion" to spatialize and objectify movement. Instead, she focused on the Bergson who saw the flow of time as the source of freedom and creativity. In chapters 2 and 3 of *Cruel Optimism*, she introduced an affective "flow model" of subjectivity that she argued was an alternative to the decision making that underlay contemporary policy making. Berlant saw in Bergson's writings a new model of affect and subjectivity that would make a difference for politics. She entitled chapter 2 of *Cruel Optimism* "The Intuitionists: History and the Affective Event." It was an obvious reference to the philosopher Bergson:

> In *Matter and Memory*, Henri Bergson writes that intuition is the work of history translated through personal memory. At the same time, I would argue, the visceral response is a trained thing, not just autonomic activity. Intuition is where affect meets history, in all of its chaos, normative ideology, and embodied practices of discipline and invention. This chapter develops, in scenes of shifting and adjustment, an account of how narratives involving the education of embodied intuition in a transforming world situation can be said to capture the drama of their historical present. (Berlant 2011, 52)

She also drew upon his book on humor, *Laughter: An Essay on the Meaning of the Comic*, but painted these affects phenomenologically and not specifically historically. How did Berlant attach cruel optimism to the historical present?

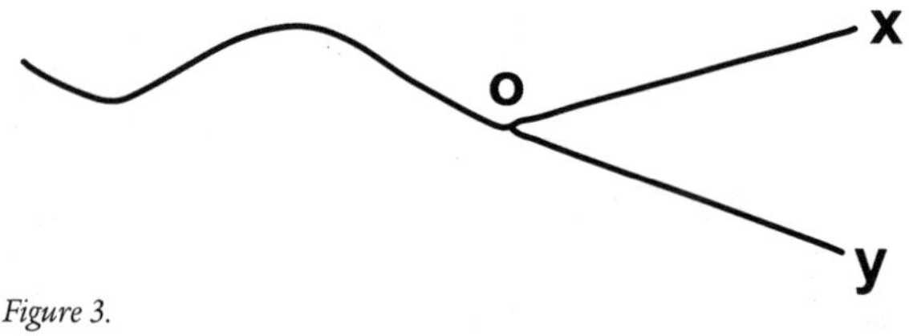

Figure 3.

The Flow of Time and Decision Making

In Time and Free Will, Bergson had accounts of affects such as desire, hope, joy and sorrow, grace, and beauty and uncovered a new model of subjectivity different from decision making. For example, he described a person who was choosing X or Y in an intersection O (figure 3), which resembled a binomial decision tree (figure 4), but had a contrasting interpretation where the self "lives and develops by means of its very hesitations, until the free action drops from it like an over-ripe fruit replacing the punctuality of the event with duration" (Bergson 1910, 176).

It was a "durative" alternative to punctuality of decision making. The decision trees, which were used to price derivatives in the Black-Scholes equation, had the same structure except they added a "metalevel" of quantitative measures for likelihoods (50%) and payoffs (+$1 and -$1).

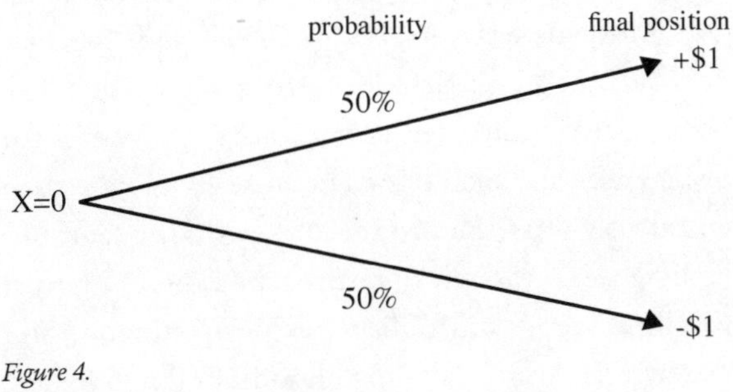

Figure 4.

Berlant saw in Bergson's writings a new model of affect and subjectivity that would make a difference in policy making. Instead of the punctuality of events of decision making, Berlant used the "situation" and "episode"; a situation was a "state of animated suspension" and a "genre of unforeclosed experience" (Berlant 2011, 5) that emphasized the multiple "flows" of duration. This elongation of the event attached itself to the "animated suspension" of apostrophe and to the historical present of cruel optimism. The extension of the event in a "horizontal dimension" was very different from the "vertical dimension" of reflexive reference in decision making under uncertainty.

Davidson, perhaps the premier architect of the belief-desire model and decision making, had constructed a "metalottery" that would act as a "metalevel" that would refer to beliefs and desires of the object level. It built upon the lottery axiom of expected utility theory taken from Von Neumann and Morgenstern's *Theory of Games and Economic Behavior*, the book that founded game theory. The object level contained quantitative measures for preferences and likelihoods because expected return and utility were the products of both; for example, if there was a monetary return, the expected return was the payoff multiplied by the likelihood, and given their estimates of likelihoods and preferences, agents had to make an "all-out" decision to form an intention to act. The metalottery resembled Tarski's metasemantic approach to truth where the object level was subjectivity before any quantitative measurement; the metalottery objectified it into likelihoods and utilities.

Quantitatively given measures of likelihoods and preferences were the bases of beliefs and desires that explained intentional action. Building upon this decision-making model, in a pathbreaking article, "Actions, Reasons, and Causes" (1980), Davidson argued that a pairing of the requisite beliefs and desires could be a causal reason for an action; this would translate expected utility theory into an empirically verifiable psychological model of beliefs and desires. Weighing one's beliefs and desires, one made a decision to form an intention that then brought about the desired action. Since beliefs and desires contained representational states, they were causally effective through the choices made, i.e., that *this* action would bring about what the actor desired *now*. Intensional and intentional states such as belief and desire became causally effective because one chose among them to make an "all-out judgment" (i.e., intention) that was both the reason and the cause for an action.

Davidson had effectively traversed the underlying structure of our folk model and fashion of speaking about subjectivity: from mental states (beliefs and desires) → mental activities (choices or decisions) → performative actions (speech acts). The belief-desire model thus provided a causal explanation of action and would link subjectivity to action and interpretation. He would expand the expected utility and game theoretic approach to the philosophy of interpretation, communication, and meaning, reinforcing the interest in analytic philosophy to provide more abstract solutions to problems of intentionality and intensionality.

Bergson was considered to have lost the Bergson-Einstein debate, but he has made a revival because of the uncertainty and volatility of quantum physics and "flow models" in business and design, mainly because of Mikhail Csikszentmihalyi's research on flow and creativity. But the most relevant connection to present academic debates was what C. P. Snow said were "two cultures," the natural sciences and the humanities. The fashions of speaking about subjectivity followed these lines, with decision making under uncertainty dominant in the social sciences, especially economics and finance, and "flow models" in the humanities.

An alternative to decision-making models was particularly important at the time because quantum entanglement ("spooky action at a distance") was all the rage in physics. Quantum entanglement might be communication beyond the speed of light, which violated Einstein's theory of relativity. John Clauser won the 2022 Nobel Prize in Physics because of quantum entanglement. In the late sixties, he was also a founder of Fundamental Fysiks, an acid-swirling and marijuana-smoking group of graduate students and young faculty in the physics department at Berkeley that became enamored with quantum entanglement and Fritz Capra, who was a member of the group and who wrote the *Tao of Physics: An Exploration of the Parallels Between Modern Physics and Eastern Mysticism*; Eastern metaphysics was dominated by flow models of *qi* (breath) and *shui* (water). Niels Bohr had the yin-yang symbol on his coat of arms when he was knighted in 1947, and Werner Heisenberg said that he was in "complete agreement" with the *Tao of Physics* (he met Capra in 1972).

Henri Bergson

In chapter 2 of *Cruel Optimism*, Berlant chose intuition and a Bergsonian flow model rather than the decision making that guided policy studies; policy making involved a sovereign agent who made decisions from a list of ordered preferences. In chapter 3, she criticized the sovereignty and instrumental reasoning of Michelle Obama's obesity policy recommendations. Bergson's theory of subjectivity did not start with logic and mathematics but from the flow of time, or what he called "duration" (durée). Duration emphasized how time was always changing from future to present to past and inherently volatile but also was the source of freedom and creativity. He distinguished between "quantitative and qualitative multiplicities," which overlapped with our senses of volatility. In fact, he seemed to see volatility everywhere, and everything was vibrating and in motion: "Matter thus resolves itself into numberless vibrations, all linked together in uninterrupted continuity, all bound up with each other, and traveling in every direction like shivers through an immense body" (Bergson 1910, 277).

Bergson's problem was how perception transforms this volatile input into images. His answer would involve his theory of duration, which was the movement of time through past, present, and future. While the quantitative notion of volatility started with the calculations of a mean and variance, Bergson started from the other extreme, the changing intensities of affects, emotions, and psychological processes before any sense of quantitative measure or comparison. These different "flows" met perception like notes in a melody, and unfolded as a "heterogenous multiplicity" in which part and whole were constantly reconstituting their relations.

We experienced affects such as joy or sorrow as flows of changing intensities whose complex modulations Bergson described in passages that would inspire writers as diverse as T. S. Eliot, Wallace Stevens, Willa Cather, William James, and Marcel Proust, as in his famous description of "an obscure desire" that started as a "feeble intensity" and became an all-enveloping "deep passion."

At the core of Bergson's account was "duration," the indexical passage of time among past, present, and future. He drew a contrast between this and what might be called "extensional time," the calendar time presupposed by mathematics and science, in which all events took place. Since he saw numbers as having an irreducible spatial component (a number was an abstraction from a coextensive collection of "objects"), quantitative multiplicities were spatializations of qualitative multiplicities, and thus mathematical time was an objectification of duration. The spatialization and objectification of duration was the root of what he called the "cinematic illusion" in cinema, mathematics, and language, which led to fundamental misunderstandings in Western philosophy concerning freedom and creativity (his main target was Kant).

Bergson argued that our experience of movement was that of a continuous, irreversible unfolding in real time, but cinema reconstructed movement from still shots, mathematics through the infinitesimal calculus, and language via its semantic structure. Deleuze would object to this characterization of cinema—like Bergson's famous example of a star gazer watching a shooting star flash across the night sky, the film viewer experienced not concatenated segments but complete movements. A similar argument might be made for language, in which discourse textual devices such as anaphora and cataphora linked sentences into a cohesive flow of text.

Bergson's account of duration was so popular among writers in the early twentieth century—he would receive the Nobel Prize for Literature in 1928—that Proust felt impelled to write that his own explorations into memory and time consciousness were independent of his best man and cousin-in-law! Bergson's allusive and evocative philosophical style was very popular with writers and artists but considered nonrigorous by analytic philosophers such as Bertrand Russell. It wasn't for lack of mathematical training; Bergson had won first prize in the prestigious Concours General for solving a mathematical problem posed by Pascal, and his philosophical books show a deep knowledge of the medicine, evolutionary theory, and psychophysics of his day.

The opening pages of *Time and Free Will* gave examples of qualitative multiplicities, all of which were affects: desire, hope, joy and sorrow, grace, beauty, and pity. In each case, he traced how qualitative changes in affective intensities change as indexical time or duration unfolds. Perhaps the most intricate was his description of the feeling experienced when watching a particularly riveting performance of a graceful dancer. In this extraordinary passage, Bergson answered a question first raised by Spinoza's theory of affects: How were complex affects and feelings built out of simpler ones? How did we start with a physical sense of the graceful movements of a dancer but end up with an account of a "moral sympathy" that would explain "the irresistible attractiveness of grace"? The answer was through the modulations of time.

Upon close reading, the piece turned out to be a rigorous analysis of the internal dynamics of grace but seemed to have a peculiar cadence and rhythm. It was a particularly graceful piece about grace that enacted in its narrative form what it analyzed. Rather than a formal rigor of logical analysis, as for Frege and philosophers of language, it had a performative aesthetic rigor in which form and content merged in the unfolding of a text that enacted what it described. A piece of "performative" narrative art, it depended on the structure of the past from future to present to past.

Bergson's Grace

Bergson considered grace an aesthetic feeling, and his analysis preceded his discussion of beauty. He gave an intricate account of how a complex feeling of grace that had religious and moral overtones was built up out of simpler feelings, starting with the physical sense produced by watching a graceful dance performance. The first portion of his analysis was purely descriptive, but in the last two lines he turned to a performative analysis in which he enacted what he described. It's not surprising that he turned to language—it's not clear how you could create complex emotions such as contempt or envy without language. However, by turning the conclusion into narrative art, Bergson foregrounded the aesthetic rather than the representational dimension of performativity; instead of creating another metasemantic level, he played with the space between indexicality and metalanguage, an example of Silverstein's metapragmatics:

1. Let us consider the simplest of them, the feeling of grace.
2. At first it is only the perception of a certain ease, a certain facility in the outward movements.
3. And as those movements are easy which prepare the way for others, we are led to

find a superior ease in the movements which can be foreseen, in the present attitudes in which future attitudes are pointed out and, as it were, prefigured.

4. If jerky movements are wanting in grace, the reason is that each of them is self-sufficient and does not announce those which are to follow.
5. If curves are more graceful than broken lines, the reason is that, while a curved line changes its direction at every moment, every new direction is indicated in the preceding one.
6. Thus the perception of ease in motion passes over into the pleasure of mastering the flow of time and of holding the future in the present.
7. A third element comes in when the graceful movements submit to a rhythm and are accompanied by music.
8. For the rhythm and measure, by allowing us to foresee to a still greater extent the movements of the dancer, make us believe that we now control them.
9. As we guess almost the exact attitude which the dancer is going to take, he seems to obey us when he really takes it: the regularity of the rhythm establishes a kind of communication between him and us, and the periodic returns of the measure are like so

many invisible threads by means of which we set in motion this imaginary puppet.

10. Indeed, if it stops for an instant, our hand in its impatience cannot refrain from making a movement, as though to push it, as though to replace it in the midst of this movement, the rhythm of which has taken complete possession of our thought and will.
11. Thus a kind of physical sympathy enters into the feeling of grace. (Bergson 1910, 11–13, numbers added)

Spinoza argued that the complex affects were logically derived from the primary affects of pleasure, pain, and desire but did not attempt to show how they were psychologically constructed. Bergson would argue that the key component was time as duration. His analysis of watching a graceful dance performance showed how the present kept the past alive by prefiguring the future in the present. But this was the very structure of duration: a graceful dance performance, by creating what choreographers call a "line" among the movements, foregrounded continuity in motion or duration. Our construction of that "line" was the basis for our pleasure in the dancer's "mastering the flow of time" (line 6) as what unfolded corresponded to our anticipation of it.

Musical accompaniment was perceptually fused to the movement but had a rhythm of its own that interacted with the line; it extended our successful anticipation of the dancer's movements to the point that our pleasure at the dancer's control was transformed into a sense of our control of his movements. The key moment was that in which "the regularity of the rhythm establishes a kind of communication between him and us" (line 9), what Rosa (2021) would call "resonance." Extending Bergson's initial description of vibrating matter turning into the perception of a graceful dancer, a graceful performance was where the different volatility spreads of the dancer and viewer were "in tune" and could match, mingle, and mix.

In the two following lines (12-13), Bergson did something extraordinary: he used the narrative unfolding of his text to enact an instance of what he was analyzing. More than fifty years before John Austin's *How to Do Things with Words* (1975), Bergson "performatively" enacted what he was describing, effectively deconstructing his own argument in *Creative Evolution* that language, cinema, and mathematics were inherently spatializing and objectifying. In his philosophy, Bergson saw language through primarily through its referential or representational function. A sentence encoded a proposition, which it broke down into discrete semantic units: nouns referred to objects, verbs to actions, and adjectives to qualities. A representation of action wasn't the action itself. His philosophy was referentially abstract, but his writing was stylistically performative and undermined his thesis about the objectifying nature of language itself.

Yet as Austin would point out, certain "performative" utterances such as "I hereby promise..." created what they referred to; a description of the act created an instance of what was described and thus blurred the lines between metalanguage and object language. As Bergson shifted from an analytic to a performative register, he enacted what he was describing:

> 12. Now, in analysing the charm of this sympathy, you will find that it pleases you through its affinity with moral sympathy, the idea of which it subtly suggests.
> 13. This last element, in which the others are merged after having in a measure ushered it in, explains the irresistible attractiveness of grace. (Bergson 1910, 13)

Narrative analysis made a distinction between the narrating voice (a personification of metalanguage) and what was narrated about (object language). In third-person narration these lines were kept apart, but in performatives and free indirect style they intersected. The shift to a performative register created an indexical intersection between describing and enacting, between the narrating voice and what was talked about, so that the discourse created an instance of what it referred to. The narrative discourse would foreground its own durative unfolding by using coreference to create a narrative "line" that mirrored the "line" created by the graceful dance movements and even suggested that the reader would be pleased by it.

The shift to a performative register was signaled in line 12 by two indexicals, the temporal deictic "now" and the second-person pronoun "you," which both referred to the ongoing discourse event.[6] The clause "in analyzing the charm of this sympathy" was both descriptive and performative, a description of what was being done and an enactment of it, which was the role of present perception in duration. This performative present indicated by "this sympathy" was then linked by anaphora to the "physical sympathy... feeling of grace" mentioned in the preceding sentence, while the rest of the sentence indexed the pleasure produced by its connection to "moral sympathy," which was prefigured in "this sympathy."

The sentence aligned the narrating and narrated-about lines so that each mirrored the temporal structure of the other through the indexical pivot signaled by the performative construction. The performative "in analyzing this sympathy" anaphorically referred to the past (the "physical sympathy" of the previous line) and the deictic reading of "this" connected it to the present moment of narration, preparing it as the presupposed referent of the indefinite third-person pronoun "it" that would cataphorically project "the charm of this sympathy" into the future discourse, where it would have an "affinity with moral sympathy." The present linked the past with a future that was immanent in it—which was the structure of duration. The analysis of a particular sympathy revealed that it was connected to a moral sympathy that it merged into but also created.

The performative structure continued in the next sentence, in which "this last element" not only indexed "moral sympathy" but also referenced "the others." Since the mixing of "physical sympathy" and "the feeling of grace" was called the "third element," "the others" referred to the previous steps in constructing the feeling of grace, the "perception of ease" and the "pleasure of mastering the flow of time" described earlier; line 6 described how "the perception of ease" was subsumed by the "pleasure of mastering time" and then both were subsumed by the moral sympathy that they also helped to usher in (line 12). The last sentence seemed to be summarizing the arguments made in the previous sections, suggesting that they were components of a "moral sympathy" that "explains the irresistible attractiveness of grace."

In perhaps the standard reading, "this last element" was anaphoric to the preceding "moral sympathy." But there was a self-referential and cataphoric reading that said that the analysis of the construction of moral sympathy out of its "others" could be applied to grace itself. In such a reading "This last element" self-referentially referred to those very words and characterized them as part of a conclusion that would explain why grace was irresistible. The process by which moral sympathy becomes constructed out of "others" was recursively applied to moral sympathy in relation to grace. Each element helped to produce and was subsumed by the next, more complex form, and in each case the transition described and enacted the unfolding of time as duration as the crucial factor.

If the anaphoric and cataphoric readings were combined, then the passage created an instance of what was described. Each step produced a feeling subsumed by the next step: "perception of ease" → "pleasure of mastering" → "moral sympathy" → "grace," which it also helped to produce. Duration or the interplay between past, present, and future played a crucial role in each transition; the temporal unfolding of duration was mirrored by the narrative play of time and coreference; in semiotic terms, the narrative structure was an "indexical icon" of what was being analyzed; it described and enacted both the presupposed (anaphoric reading) and the creative dimensions (cataphoric readings). The irresistibility of grace was made up of "moral sympathy" and the "others," including the other elements and the supporting analyses, all of which presaged their role in creating the irresistible attractiveness of grace.

The conclusion thus enacted what it described: it "said" that all the steps and elements had a common performative principle in which they were subsumed by what they produced, and that was what explained "the irresistible attractiveness of grace." But extending the principle of argument that was immanent in the structure of the analysis and applying it to moral sympathy itself would show why grace was irresistible—moral sympathy would be pleasing because of its affinity to grace, by which it was subsumed but also produced.

The "logic" of this performative unfolding was completely rigorous, but it was neither dialectical nor formal. Duration was a qualitative alternative to the quantitative measures of the "belief-desire" model of expected utility theory and instead used the internal structure of the flow of time; it played with the "spread" between indexicality and metaindexicality. Each succeeding step presupposed the previous one, which also created it. It was governed by creating a performative analogy between the narrative unfolding of the analysis and what was analyzed so that the "force" of the former animated the latter. What was special about grace was that even though duration was the dynamic motor of all affects and feelings, grace foregrounded the temporal structure of duration by creating a "line" that can be sensed through the qualitative changes of intensity. As an example of an aesthetic feeling, the construction of grace was the embodiment of a performative aesthetic principle in which a flow of forms displayed and enacted the force that produced it.

Conclusion

Bergson's analysis of grace showed how more complex affects could be created of simpler ones. It used no quantitative measures, only qualitative ones involving the flow of time, like linguistic discourse did with anaphora, cataphora, and coreference. In chapters 2 and 3 of *Cruel Optimism*, Berlant saw the "flow" model as an alternative to the punctuality of decision making, which emphasized agent-centered means-end rationality, chopping psychological processes into discrete events so their agents could control them. She complained that means-end rationality was behind contemporary policy thinking and sovereignty: "in linking and inflating consciousness, invention, and *decision* or *event* it has provided an alibi for hygienic governmentality and justified moralizing against inconvenient human activity" (Berlant 2011, 96-97; my emphasis).

The belief-desire model and decision making under uncertainty were the dominant models in the social sciences, especially economics and finance; game theory was a widely used model for strategic thinking and policy decisions. Binomial trees became the rage in finance to price derivatives; with Clinton's deregulation of derivatives, monetary wealth flew into finance and derivatives catalyzed the expansion of neoliberal capitalism until the Great Recession of 2007-2009, overlapping with Berlant's writing of the book.

Cruel Optimism looked at the affective structures of neoliberalism as it consolidated the two decades from 1990 to the end of the Great Recession; it included several European films (by the Dardenne brothers and Lauren Cantet), indicating that the disaffections of neoliberalism weren't confined to their origins in Thatcher's England and Reagan's United States. Berlant saw neoliberalism as a form of decision making. However, the philosophical debates about neoliberalism in the United States were set by John Rawls and Robert Nozick, who derived their contrasting positions for distributional justice and the free market from game theory. Decision making spread to moral philosophy and would spread to the philosophy of language through works such as

Davidson's philosophy of action and through David Lewis, who wrote *Convention*, which started with Thomas Schelling's game-theoretic account of coordination games. A formalized belief-desire model with quantitative measures quickly became the ideal model of subjectivity in the social sciences.

Berlant saw in Bergson's writings a new model of affect and subjectivity that would make a difference in policy making. Instead of the punctuality of events of decision making, Berlant posited the "situation" and "episode"; a situation was a "state of animated suspension" and a "genre of unforeclosed experience" (Berlant 2011, 5), which emphasized the multiple "flows" of duration. This elongation of the event attached itself to the "animated suspension" of apostrophe and to the historical present of cruel optimism. The extension of the event in a "horizontal dimension" meant slowing down the flow of time to see the micromovements of volatility and creativity; it was very different from the "vertical dimension" of reflexive reference in decision making under uncertainty.

Berlant criticized decision making and means-end rationality policy decisions in favor of affect and subjectivity. She also criticized Michelle Obama's neoliberal recommendations for child diet and nutrition, saying that present policies were in a "rhetoric of policy (that) require that one subscribe to a model of institutional and agency that frames the adjustment as a dramatic event," emphasizing the sovereignty of agency and the punctuality of the event. This rhetoric appealed to an "obesity epidemic" where we had "to get the fat (the substance and the people) under control" (Berlant 2011, 103-4) rather than "seeing eating as a kind of self-medication through self-interruption" (Berlant 2011, 115), which emphasized the prolongation of the event into a durative situation with episodic recurrences.

An unlikely ally for Berlant appeared in the economist John Maynard Keynes, who might have favored her approach to affect and subjectivity. When describing the behavior of the stock market, he objected to the statistical approaches to expected return in favor of "animal spirits":

> Most, probably, of our decisions to do something positive, the full consequences of which will be drawn out over many days to come, can only be taken as a result of animal spirits—of a spontaneous urge to action rather than inaction, and not as the outcome of a weighted average of quantitative benefits multiplied by quantitative probabilities. (Keynes 1936, 161)

Animal spirits were the focus of the hottest developing field in economics: behavioral economics, discovered by Amos Tversky and Daniel Kahneman. It started with a question that Davidson didn't consider: Why didn't people follow the dictates and expectations of expected utility theory? Why didn't they behave rationally, as if they were utility maximizers? Tversky and Kahneman gave a series of local but systematic explanations such as heuristics, rules of thumb, anchoring, and affective biases to explain why people were "irrational." Behavioral economics left a space for affect and animal spirits and touched upon flow as an empirical phenomenon.

In a best-selling classic of behavioral economics, *Thinking, Fast and Slow*, Kahneman referenced Csikszentmihalyi's research when he recounted walking in the Berkeley Woods in a state of "flow," when he enjoyed his most creative thinking. Of course, capitalism was the economic system that depended upon innovation, to produce more relative surplus value; innovation was subsumed by profit. However, economic flow models in capitalism gave a romantic interlude of maximum creativity without any effort, which was why they were so popular in business and design schools. The standard business question was how to make a profit out of the flow of creativity that seems to be autotelic. If people commodify their innovations, they will have more material wealth without worrying about their labor because it doesn't seem like hard work.

In his analysis of grace, Bergson gave the first picture of the dynamics of duration. He looked into the flow of time to give a performative account of grace without any mathematical measures but only the flow from future to present to past, contrasting with the belief-desire model of decision making dominant in the natural and social sciences. Berlant objected to means-ends rationality behind policy thinking, which fundamentally misunderstood affect, intuition, and duration. By prolonging the event, Berlant tried to see the immanent creative potential of flows of affect. Treating affect as firmly grounded in the historical present, Berlant selected apostrophe and free indirect style from the continuum of rhetorical tropes that Silverstein had discovered; she would use them to translate affect into cruel optimism and what Postone would call the contradictory nature of relative surplus value or technological innovation. If quantitative and mathematical time represented abstract labor and duration represented the qualitative dimensions of concrete labor time, then the contradiction of objective and subjective perspectives on time has driven the dynamics of relative surplus value and neoliberal capitalism. As we face an AI-generated mass unemployment, are we in a new, qualitatively different capitalism where we commodify the volatile flow of innovation without the input of human labor?

Endnotes

1. Foucault traced the concept of human capital back to the Chicago economics department. However, the wealth of neoliberalism was produced by derivative finance, which was catalyzed by the Black-Scholes model for pricing derivatives. This was discovered by Fisher Black and Myron Scholes from the Chicago School of Business, which founded much of contemporary finance.
2. *Metapragmatics* has a general unmarked meaning versus a restricted meaning opposed to metasemantics.
3. Frege's distinction of sense and reference and Austin's speech act theory could be considered dependent on our Whorfian "fashion of speaking" about subjectivity and time in SAE languages.
4. According to Daniel Kwan, one of the directors of *Everything Everywhere All at Once*, he was influenced by the modal realism of David Lewis.
5. Locution was based upon Frege's *logical* distinction between sense and reference; illocution was based upon performatives, for which Austin tried to find a *grammatical* definition, and "persuade" was a perlocutionary verb that described the traditional definition of *rhetoric*. Speech act theory embodied the classical distinctions among grammar (illocution), logic (locution), and rhetoric (persuasion).
6. The original French: "Il entrera donc dans le sentiment du gracieux une espèce de sympathie physique, et en analysant le charme de cette sympathie, vous verrez qu'elle vous plaît elle-même par son affinité avec la sympathie morale, dont elle vous suggère subtilement l'idée." Although "now" does not appear, the performative reading is maintained by "en analysant" ("in analysing") and three references to "vous" (instead of "on").

References

Anderson, Benedict. 1991. *Imagined Communities: Reflections on the Origins and Spread of Nationalism*. New York: Verso Press.

Austin, John. 1975. *How to Do Things with Words*. Cambridge, MA: Harvard University Press.

Benveniste, Emile. 1972. Trans. Elizabeth Meek. *Problems in General Linguistics*. Miami: University of Miami Press.

Bergson, Henri. 1910. Trans. F. L. Pogson. *Time and Free Will: An Essay on the Immediate Data of Consciousness*. London: George Allen & Unwin.

Berlant, Lauren. 2011. *Cruel Optimism*. Durham, NC: Duke University Press.

Csikszentmihalyi, Mihaly. 1996. *Creativity: Flow and the Psychology of Discovery and Invention*. New York: Harper Perennial.

Davidson, Donald. 1980. "Action, Reasons, and Causes." In *Essays on Actions and Events*, 3–19. Oxford: Clarendon Press.

De Man, Paul. 1979. *Allegories of Reading: Figural Language in Rousseau, Nietzsche, Rilke, and Proust*. New Haven, CT: Yale University Press.

Derman, Emanuel. 2023. "A Stylized History of Volatility." SSRN papers. http://dx.doi.org/10.2139/ssrn.4297590/.

Derrida, Jacques. 1974. *Of Grammatology*. Trans. Gayatri Spivak. Baltimore, MD: Johns Hopkins University Press.

The Economist. 2022. "When Albert Einstein and Henri Bergson Rowed About Time." https://www.economist.com/culture/when-albert-einstein-and-henri-bergson-rowed-about-time/21808591.

Frege, Gottlieb. 1962. "Sense and Reference." In *Philosophical Writings*, ed. M. Black and P. T. Geach, 56–78. Oxford: Blackwell.

Gingerich, Jon. 2012. "The Benefits of Free Indirect Discourse." *Lit Reactor*. litreactor.com/columns/the-benefits-of-free-indirect-discourse.

Habermas, Jürgen. 1989. *The Structural Transformation of the Public Sphere An Inquiry into a Category of Bourgeois Society*. Trans. Thomas Burger. Cambridge, MA: MIT Press.

Jakobson, Roman. 1960. "Closing Statement: Linguistics and Poetics." In *Style in Language*, ed. Thomas Sebeok, 350–77. Cambridge, MA, and New York: MIT Press and Wiley.

—. 1985. *Verbal Art, Verbal Sign, Verbal Time*. Ed. Krystyna Pomorska and Stephen Rudy. Oxford: Basil Blackwell.

—. 1987. "Linguistics and Poetics." In *Language in Literature*, ed. Krystyna Pomorska and Stephen Rudy, 62–94. Cambridge, MA: Harvard University Press.

—. 1990. "Two Aspects of Language and Two Types of Aphasic Disturbances." In *On Language*, ed. Linda Waugh and Monique Monville-Burston, 115–33. Cambridge, MA: Harvard University Press.

Johnson, Barbara. 1986. "Apostrophe, Animation, and Abortion." *Diacritics* (Spring): 29–47.

Keynes, John Maynard. 1936. *The General Theory of Employment, Interest and Money*. London: Macmillan.

Lee, Benjamin. 1997. *Talking Heads: Language, Metalanguage, and the Semiotics of Subjectivity*. Durham, NC: Duke University Press.

Lucey, Michael and Thomas McEnaney, eds. 2017. Special Issue on "Language-In-Use and the Literary Artifact." *Representations* 137, no. 1.

Marx, Karl. 1977. *Capital*. Volume I. Trans. Ben Fowkes. New York: Vintage.

Ngai, Sianne. 2020. *Theory of the Gimmick: Aesthetic Judgement and Capitalist Form*. Cambridge, MA: Harvard University Press.

Postone, Moishe. 1993. *Labor, Time, and Social Domination: A Reinterpretation of Marx's Critical Theory*. Cambridge, MA: Cambridge University Press.

Robbins, Joel. 2001. "Ritual Communication and Linguistic Ideology." *Current Anthropology* 42, no. 5 (December): 591–614.

Rosa, Hartmut. 2021. *Resonance: A Sociology of Our Relationship to the World*. New York: Polity Press.

Sapir, Edward. 1921. New York: Harcourt, Brace, & World.

Silverstein, Michael. 1976a. "Hierarchy of Features and Ergativity." In R. M. W. Dixon, ed., *Grammatical Categories in Australian Languages*, ed. R. M. W. Dixon, 112–71. Canberra, ACT: Australian Institute of Aboriginal [and Torres Straits Islander] Studies.

—. 1976b. "Shifters, Linguistic Categories, and Cultural Description." In *Meaning in Anthropology*, ed. Henry Selby and Keith Basso, 11–55. Albuquerque: University of New Mexico Press.

—. 1981a. "Case-marking and the Nature of Language." *Australian Journal of Linguistics* 1: 227–47.

—. 1981b. Unpublished paper. "Metaforces of Power in Traditional Oratory."

—. 1987. "Three Faces of Function: Preliminaries to a Psychology of Language." In *Social and Functional Approaches to Language and Thought*, ed. Maya Hickmann. New York: Academic Press.

—. 2000. "Whorfianism and the Linguistic Imagination of Nationality." In *Regimes of Language: Ideologies, Politics, and Identities*, ed. Paul Kroskrity, 85–138. Santa Fe: School of American Research Press.

—. 2023. *Language in Culture: Lectures on the Social Semiotics of Language*. Ed. E. Summerson Carr, Susan Gal, and Constantine Nakassis. Cambridge: Cambridge University Press.

Sperber, Dan. 2008. "Claude Levi-Strauss, a Precursor?" *European Journal of Sociology* XLIX, no. 2: 309–14.

Vendler, Zeno. 1972. *Res Cogitans*. Ithaca, NY: Cornell University Press.

Whorf, Benjamin Lee. 1956. *Language, Thought, and Reality: Selected Writings of Benjamin Lee Whorf*. Cambridge, MA: MIT Press.

Also available from Prickly Paradigm Press:

1
Waiting for Foucault, Still
Marshall Sahlins

2
War of the Worlds: What about Peace?
Bruno Latour

3
Against Bosses, Against Oligarchies: A Conversation with Richard Rorty
Richard Rorty, Derek Nystrom, and Kent Puckett

4
The Secret Sins of Economics
Deirdre McCloskey

5
New Consensus for Old: Cultural Studies from Left to Right
Thomas Frank

6
Talking Politics: The Substance of Style from Abe to "W"
Michael Silverstein

7
Revolt of the Masscult
Chris Lehmann

8
The Companion Species Manifesto: Dogs, People, and Significant Otherness
Donna Haraway

9
9/12: New York After
Eliot Weinberger

10
On the Edges of Anthropology (Interviews)
James Clifford

11
The Thanksgiving Turkey Pardon, the Death of Teddy's Bear, and the Sovereign Exception of Guantánamo
Magnus Fiskesjö

12
The Root of Roots: Or, How Afro-American Anthropology Got its Start
Richard Price and Sally Price

13
What Happened to Art Criticism?
James Elkins

14
Fragments of an Anarchist Anthropology
David Graeber

15
Enemies of Promise: Publishing, Perishing, and the Eclipse of Scholarship
Lindsay Waters

16
The Empire's New Clothes: Paradigm Lost, and Regained
Harry Harootunian

17
Intellectual Complicity: The State and Its Destructions
Bruce Kapferer

18
The Hitman's Dilemma: Or, Business, Personal and Impersonal
Keith Hart

19
The Law in Shambles
Thomas Geoghegan

20

The Stock Ticker and the Superjumbo: How The Democrats Can Once Again Become America's Dominant Political Party
Rick Perlstein

21

Museum, Inc.: Inside the Global Art World
Paul Werner

22

Neo-Liberal Genetics: The Myths and Moral Tales of Evolutionary Psychology
Susan McKinnon

23

Phantom Calls: Race and the Globalization of the NBA
Grant Farred

24

The Turn of the Native
Eduardo Viveiros de Castro, Flávio Gordon, and Francisco Araújo

25

The American Game: Capitalism, Decolonization, World Domination, and Baseball
John D. Kelly

26

"Culture" and Culture: Traditional Knowledge and Intellectual Rights
Manuela Carneiro da Cunha

27

Reading Legitimation Crisis in Tehran: Iran and the Future of Liberalism
Danny Postel

28

Anti-Semitism and Islamophobia: Hatreds Old and New in Europe
Matti Bunzl

29

Neomedievalism, Neoconservatism, and the War on Terror
Bruce Holsinger

30

Understanding Media: A Popular Philosophy
Dominic Boyer

31

Pasta and Pizza
Franco La Cecla

32

The Western Illusion of Human Nature: With Reflections on the Long History of Hierarchy, Equality, and the Sublimation of Anarchy in the West, and Comparative Notes on Other Conceptions of the Human Condition
Marshall Sahlins

33

Time and Human Language Now
Jonathan Boyarin and Martin Land

34

American Counterinsurgency: Human Science and the Human Terrain
Roberto J. González

35

The Counter-Counterinsurgency Manual: Or, Notes on Demilitarizing American Society
Network of Concerned Anthropologists

36

Are the Humanities Inconsequent? Interpreting Marx's Riddle of the Dog
Jerome McGann

37

The Science of Passionate Interests: An Introduction to Gabriel Tarde's Economic Anthropology
Bruno Latour and Vincent Antonin Lépinay

38

Pacification and its Discontents
Kurt Jacobsen

39

An Anthropological Theory of the Corporation
Ira Bashkow

40

The Great Debate About Art
Roy Harris

41

The Inconstancy of the Indian Soul: The Encounter of Catholics and Cannibals in 16th-Century Brazil
Eduardo Viveiros de Castro

42

The Ecology of Others: Anthropology and the Question of Nature
Philippe Descola

43

Pastoral in Palestine
Neil Hertz

44

The Culture of Ethics
Franco La Cecla and Piero Zanini

45

2001 and Counting: Kubrick, Nietzsche, and Anthropology
Bruce Kapferer

46

Data: Now Bigger and Better!
Edited by Tom Boellstorff and Bill Maurer

47

Jean-Pierre Vernant: From the Maquis to the Polis
Jean-Pierre Vernant, edited and with preface by François Hartog

48

Confucius Institutes: Academic Malware
Marshall Sahlins

49

The Science of Myths and Vice Versa
Gregory Schrempp

50

Community of Scholars, Community of Teachers
Judith Shapiro

51

"Man—with Variations": Interviews with Franz Boas and Colleagues, 1937
Joseph Mitchell, edited and with an introduction by Robert Brightman

52

Making Trouble: Surrealism and the Human Sciences
Derek Sayer

53

Complicities: The People's Republic of China in Global Capitalism
Arif Dirlik

54

What the Foucault?
Marshall Sahlins

55

Populism Left and Right
Éric Fassin

56

Making Kin not Population
Edited by Adele E. Clarke
and Donna Haraway

57

The Gift Paradigm:
A Short Introduction to the
Anti-utilitarian Movement
in the Social Sciences
Alain Caillé

58

Kinds of Value:
An Experiment in Modal Anthropology
Paul Kockelman

59

The Jewish Question Again
Edited by Joyce Dalsheim
and Gregory Starrett

60

Presence and Social Obligation:
An Essay on the Share
James Ferguson

61

Can a Liberal Be a Chief?
Can a Chief Be a Liberal?
Some Thoughts on an Unfinished
Business of Colonialism
Olúfẹ́mi Táíwò

62

Subaltern Studies 2.0
Milinda Banerjee
and Jelle J.P. Wouters

63

Grievance: In Fragments
Grant Farred

64

Last Words:
Large Language Models
and the AI Apocalypse
Paul Kockelman